The Proceedings of GREAT Day

2016

SUNY Geneseo

Geneseo, NY

About GREAT Day and
The Proceedings of GREAT Day

Geneseo Recognizing Excellence, Achievement, & Talent is a college-wide symposium celebrating the creative and scholarly endeavors of our students. In addition to recognizing the achievements of our students, the purpose of GREAT Day is to help foster academic excellence, encourage professional development, and build connections within the community.

Established in 2009, *The Proceedings of GREAT Day* journal compiles and publishes promising student work presented at SUNY Geneseo's GREAT Day symposium. The projects, presentations, and research included here represent the academic rigor, multidisciplinary study, and creativity of the students taking part in the SUNY Geneseo GREAT Day symposium.

Editors: Marley DeRosia, Geneseo Class of 2018

Brendan Mahoney, Geneseo Class of 2018

Publishing Supervisor: Daniel Ross, Academic Excellence Librarian, Milne Library

Editorial Consultant: Sheryl Larson-Rhodes, First-Year Experience Librarian, Milne Library

Production Manager: Allison Brown, Digital Publishing Services Manager, Milne Library

Publisher: Milne Library, SUNY Geneseo

These proceedings can be accessed online at greatjournal.geneseo.edu

Acknowledgments

SPECIAL THANKS TO:

Patty Hamilton-Rodgers, GREAT Day Coordinator

Leah Root, Publishing & Web Services Developer

GREAT Day is funded by the Office of the Provost,
the Student Association, Campus Auxiliary Services,
and the Jack '76 and Carol '76 Kramer Endowed Lectureship.

The GREAT Day Website: http://www.geneseo.edu/great_day

Table of Contents

An Interview with Patty Hamilton-Rodgers, GREAT Day Coordinator   1
Brendan Mahoney

An Interview with Dr. Jennifer Katz, Professor of Psychology   3
Brendan Mahoney

Effect of Exposure to a Safe Zone Symbol on Perceptions of Campus Climate for LGBTQ Students   4
Dillon Federici and Jennifer Katz

A Reflection with Brendan Mahoney, *The Proceedings of GREAT Day* Editor   12

Kill or Be Killed: Seeing the Middle East as a Threat to the Western World   13
Katherine Zaslavsky

An Interview with Dr. Steve Derne, Professor of Sociology   28
Brendan Mahoney

Near-Death Experience and the Mystic Path   29
Felicia Ryan

An Interview with Taylor Powers, Student Author   33
Brendan Mahoney

Non-Native Speaker Perception of Native Speaker Dialect Authenticity and Implications for Pedagogy   34
Taylor Powers

An Interview with Kaitlyn Morgan, Student Author   40
Brendan Mahoney

Not Just for "That Kind of Mom": An Ethnographic Analysis of the Perceived Benefits of Childbirth Doulas in Rochester, New York   41
Kaitlyn Morgan

An Interview with Dr. Tze-Ki Hon, Professor of History   52
Brendan Mahoney

"New China, Great Olympics": A Historical Study of the 2008 Beijing Olympic Games as a Spectacle that Promoted Chinese National Strength on an International Stage   53
Thomas F. Garrity

Fist of Fury or *Drunken Master*: Masculinity, National Identity, and Contemporary China   61
Peter Benson

First Flame: An Interview with the Creators   70
Marley DeRosia

First Flame   76
Mariposa Fernandez, Nana Boakye, Elizabeth Boateng, Seung Kim, Jenny Soudachanh, Skyler Alexander Susnick, and Jawad (Momo) Tazari, Glenn McClure, Dr. Mark Broomfield

An Interview with Patty Hamilton-Rodgers, GREAT Day Coordinator

Brendan Mahoney

What makes GREAT Day great?

Patty: One thing is the numbers. Last year we had 938 students participate in GREAT Day. This year we'd love a thousand, but…that's obviously enviable. I've talked with people who work on similar programs at other colleges about how well-received GREAT Day is—they are in awe. SUNY does an undergraduate research conference for all the SUNYs and I was talking with one of the organizers of that, telling her about GREAT Day, and she thought it was amazing. I've actually had phone calls from Farmingdale and Brockport about how we run GREAT Day, and they find it enviable as well.

I think another great thing about GREAT Day is that we're all-encompassing. It's not just research and presentations. We've got the music festival, a couple years ago we partnered with GCAB to do the Battle of the Artists, Guerilla poetry had a big display last year out on the quad, GEO did a dumpster dive…if anybody comes in we try to make it work. Everything that makes Geneseo great makes GREAT Day great.

What impact do you think GREAT Day has on our campus culture?

Patty: It's funny you should ask that—there's a national organization called The Council for Undergraduate Research that's having an undergraduate research program director's conference this summer and I've submitted a presentation on GREAT Day, so I did a little homework on this…since GREAT Day started, the number of students involved in undergraduate research has doubled and the amount of funding for undergraduate research has tripled. So that's one very real impact of GREAT Day. There aren't a lot of other variations in that ten years either, so I really think that speaks volumes for GREAT Day. I do a follow-up survey every year for people who participated—and there are always those people who will only tell me there weren't enough selections for the free sandwiches—but the people who really take the time to be mindful of their answers talk about how proud they are to present on GREAT Day and how much it means to them for people outside their discipline to see them presenting.

Why do you think it's important to have a space where people can present their ideas?

Patty: I think that it's important for people to share their work. If you're talking about basic research, part of research is telling people what you learned, what you found out. I always list in the GREAT Day program if students' presentations have been selected to be presented elsewhere, because a lot of our presentations are picked by national conferences. You know, I think at Geneseo we embrace learning on a grand scale. Part of learning is sharing your knowledge. One of the things that just blows me away every year at GREAT Day is that I can stand in the middle of the poster session—and I'm not a science person—but I can stand there with a physics student and they can explain what they've learned in a way that I can understand. They're very good about that. I think our students take a lot of pride in the work they do, and so being able to show it off is a way to express that. It's great to learn something, but it's also such an amazing feeling for Geneseo students to show someone else what they learned.

And why is it important to share knowledge?

Patty: I mean…we're an educational institution, and a shared knowledge is part of what makes our students more complete people going forward in their lives. I think another thing that makes our students more complete is the ability to present your ideas at all. I mean I was a COMN major so I can get up in front of a group and talk about anything, but not everybody has that skill and I think that's something else that makes GREAT Day important. That's one of the most basic benefits Geneseo can provide. I think, when you learn something or complete a project, the next step is to share that, right? We all want to take a little pride in our work, brag a little, right?

What presentations did you go to last year, and to which ones do you wish you went to?

Patty: Oh sweety…[pulls out program guide from last year] I wish I'd gone to all of these. I mean I always make it around the poster session, so I find that I can scope out the posters. There's actually a poster hanging up in the other room about art that I absolutely loved. The students never came back to collect it so I just hung it on my wall. I also try to make it to at least one of the concurrent presentations, and it will often be one by a student that I know. But I'd love to go to so many more. People will say to me afterwards that there was so much they didn't get to see and that we should do this for two days instead of one, and all kinds of stuff like that…there are so many I'd love to get to that I just can't see. The Edgar Fellows—the Honors Program—they are always present and those are always so fascinating. They've done their homework, to be cute. Mock Trial, a student organization, does a presentation that I went to one year. Just to see what they did… it was very cool. I always want to go to all of them, and I always only make it to one or two. But it's nice to just walk around the poster session. The ones that jumped out at me…there was one student who did a whole presentation on buildings that have grass on the roof. That was fascinating. There was one student—a music student—who did work one year on some musical archives that we have in our library. That was really cool as well. Physics has great posters, biology has great posters…to go back to one of your earlier questions, every department is represented at GREAT Day and I think it's that diversity that makes the event so special—and it's reflective of the entire college. There are obviously some students doing research that I don't understand. But if you walk up to a chemistry student on GREAT Day, they can tell you what they're doing in layman's terms. I always wish I could walk up to everyone and have them do that.

Did you have a single, favorite moment from GREAT Day last year?

Patty: Last year's GREAT Day speaker was stellar. He was Brother Guy Consolmagno, and he's the Director of the Vatican Observatory. His interaction with students was wonderful. During the final poster session he did a book signing, and the way he talked to students during it—I liked that a lot. I mean…the man knows the Pope! He's known the past several Popes, and you don't have to be Catholic to appreciate how important that is. Seeing someone like that here at our school and talking to our kids…that was really cool.

Great, well I think that's pretty much everything I wanted to talk about.

Patty: Well, alright. Wait, where's my Easy Button? [finds and presses it] That was easy.

An Interview with Dr. Jennifer Katz, Professor of Psychology

Brendan Mahoney

What's great for you about GREAT Day?

Katz: GREAT Day positively disrupts our weekly schedules and routines. On this day, members of the community are given time and space to learn from the interesting and important scholarly work that engages so many students on our campus. Every year, the breadth of different topics being investigated amazes me—even within my own department. Outside of psychology, across other disciplines, it's exciting to learn about different ways of asking scholarly questions and ways to find answers to those questions. I also enjoy the diverse, thought-provoking musical, dance, and other artistic exhibitions. Our campus is full of talent.

What impact do you think GREAT Day has on our campus culture?

Katz: GREAT Day signifies Geneseo's investment in scholarship and creative work in and out of the classroom. GREAT Day projects allow students to explore topics that fascinate them, and this exploration positively contributes to an environment in which people love to learn. Scholarly and creative projects also can inspire meaningful connections with others. I've developed wonderful longstanding relationships with undergraduate researchers by working together on research.

Why does undergraduate research in general matter to you?

Katz: As an undergraduate student, I was fortunate to work with a medical sociology research team. I understood for the first time that even professional scholars had more questions than answers. I learned that an important part of the research process, perhaps even the most important part, was to formulate questions that were important to try to answer. I discovered it was possible to be a consumer of knowledge while also helping to produce knowledge. In these ways, undergraduate research changed my life. It inspired me to attend graduate school, to pursue a career as an academic clinical psychologist, and to continuously learn about important issues, to ask questions, and to look for answers.

What's your interest in the specific topic being researched in the following paper?

Katz: The specific topic of this project was based on brainstorming and collaboration with Dillon Federici. Dillon wanted to pursue a research question that might have positive implications for student well-being. As a clinical psychologist, I've long been interested in conditions and contexts that affect individual well-being. One such condition is a stigmatized social identity. A person who is devalued on the basis of their individual attributes (such as being LGBTQ) or experiences (such as sexual assault victimization) is at risk for poorer well-being. Poorer well-being cannot be understood merely at the individual level—social and institutional norms shape our experiences that affect our well-being. Because of this interaction of the individual and the environment, initiatives such as Safe Zones may benefit individuals and our broader community. In combination, Dillon's interests, my interests, and the recent local resurgence of Safe Zone trainings led us to formulate our specific research question: does exposure to a Safe Zone symbol improve perceptions of the campus climate?

Effect of Exposure to a Safe Zone Symbol on Perceptions of Campus Climate for LGBTQ Students

Dillon Federici and Jennifer Katz

ABSTRACT

This study investigated student perceptions of campus climate after brief exposure to a Safe Zone symbol. Undergraduates (N = 265; 78% female, 80% white, 14% LGBTQ, 18-23 years old) were randomly assigned to read an excerpt from a fictitious course syllabus that either did or did not feature a Safe Zone symbol. Afterwards, participants rated campus climate characteristics for LGBTQ students. Participants who viewed a Safe Zone symbol reported more positive campus climate characteristics for LGBTQ students than those who did not view a Safe Zone symbol. Exposure to the symbol was not associated with perceptions of negative campus climate characteristics. The current results provide initial experimental evidence that displaying Safe Zone symbols can promote inclusive, accepting perceptions of the campus community.

In recent years, scholars and the general public alike have increasingly focused on the implicit and explicit forms of bias experienced by individuals who identify as lesbian, gay, bisexual, transgender, queer or questioning (LGBTQ). Unfortunately, youth who identify as LGBTQ are at increased risk for school-based bullying and associated outcomes such as poor school grades, depression, loneliness, hostility towards others, substance abuse, and suicide attempts (Kosciw, Greytak, Palmer, & Boesen, 2014). Some of these stressors and outcomes seem directly related to campus climate, defined as "attitudes of other members of the campus community toward GLBT persons and issues" (Brown, Clarke, Gortmaker, & Robinson-Keilig, 2004, p. 8). Unfortunately, students who identify as LGBTQ tend to perceive school climates as both less positive and more negative than students who do not identify as LGBTQ (Brown et al., 2004; Yost & Gilmore, 2011). Clearly, campus-based initiatives to support these youth are needed.

Fortunately, several studies suggest that explicitly inclusive campus policies and programs have a positive impact on the larger campus climate. A comprehensive review of such policies and programs in U.S. high schools and colleges found beneficial effects of "teaching about LGBT issues in classroom curriculum, staff development related to LGBT issues, student support clubs, inclusive antidiscrimination policies, and...showing support through visual displays, such as posters, flyers or media" (Black, Fedewa, & Gonzalez, 2012, p. 324). These interventions were associated with improved psychological and social outcomes for all students. Furthermore, compared to LGBTQ students who attended schools without inclusive policies or programs, LGBTQ students in schools with inclusive policies and programs reported feeling more comfortable with their sexual identities, more empowered, less harassed, and also reported fewer instances of skipping class due to feeling unsafe. The review also suggested that all students, regardless of their sexual orientation or gender identity, felt more comfortable with faculty known to have participated in Safe Zone, a specific LGBTQ supportive program, than with faculty who did not (Black et al., 2012).

Safe Zone programs are a safe school initiative developed to support individuals who are LGBTQ in both K-12 (e.g., Ratts et al., 2013) and college settings (e.g., Evans, 2002). In general, such programs operate by identifying volunteers interested in promoting inclusivity and support for those who are LGBTQ. Volunteers typically participate in a training program aimed toward increasing their cultural competence regarding LGBTQ issues (e.g., Finkel, Storaasli, Bandele, & Schaefer, 2003). After training, volunteers show support for people who are LGBTQ by displaying some variation of a rainbow symbol and the words, "Safe Zone." For example, instructors, counselors, administrators, or coaches might post Safe Zone symbols on their office doors to let passersby know that these offices are "safe spaces" where LGBTQ-related topics can be openly discussed.

Few studies have evaluated the impact of Safe Zone programs on campus climate. The available research suggests that such programs promote favorable outcomes. In an ethnographic study, implementation of a Safe Zone program on a college campus positively contributed to feelings of safety, inclusiveness, and support among students and staff that identified as LGBTQ (Evans, 2002). Furthermore, students who did not identify as LGBTQ reported increased personal awareness and inclination to seek further education related to LGBTQ issues (Evans, 2002). Similar positive results were reported in a study of a Safe Schools Survey Program in high schools; this program was found to be associated with a greater perceived "safety, tolerance, and atmosphere of respect" (Szalacha, 2003, p. 62) for LGBTQ students. However, reactions to Safe Zone programs and materials did vary in these past studies. Some members of the college community who did not identify as LGBTQ felt indifferent toward or even offended by Safe Zone materials (Evans, 2002). Likewise, youth who identified as LGBTQ reported less favorable campus climates for LGBTQ students than youth who did not identify as LGBTQ (Szalacha, 2003). This finding suggests that some climate problems may not be visible to those who are cisgender and heterosexual.

Although past studies are mostly encouraging, a causal relationship between Safe Zone programming and perceptions of a positive climate for LGBTQ students has not yet been established to our knowledge. External concurrent factors associated with the introduction of a Safe Zone program, such as administrative willingness to implement programs, general commitment by faculty and staff members to inclusiveness, could provide an alternative explanation for the apparent positive influence of Safe Zone programs on both actual and perceived campus cli-

mate in past ethnographic and correlational research. Regardless of external factors that may affect perceptions of climate generally, a major goal of Safe Zone programs is to create a visible presence of allies who display the Safe Zone symbol (Ratts et al., 2013). Given the importance of the symbols as visual cues of acceptance and support, the primary purpose of the present study was to examine the potential impact of exposure to Safe Zone symbols on undergraduate students' perceptions of campus climate for LGBTQ students.

Although no studies have examined the impact of exposure to Safe Zone symbols on participants' perceptions of campus climate, experimental research investigating other types of symbols suggests that even brief exposure can have powerful effects on attitudes and behaviors. In one study, pictures of school-related images influenced school budget voting behavior (Berger, Meredith, & Wheeler, 2008) and, in another, an image of the American flag significantly affected political beliefs up to eight months after exposure to the symbol (Carter, Ferguson, & Hassin, 2011). Expanding on these past studies showing that symbols affect viewers' attitudes and behavior, in the current study, exposure to a Safe Zone symbol was expected to be associated with more favorable perceptions of campus climate for LGBTQ students. This was the primary study hypothesis tested in the current research.

METHOD

Participants

Participants were 265 undergraduate students from a small liberal arts college in the northeastern United States. About 78% identified as female (cisgender or transgender), 21% identified as male (cisgender or transgender), and 1% identified outside the gender binary. Participants' ages ranged from 18 to 23 (M = 18.91, SD = 0.98). The majority of participants identified as White (79.6%), followed by Asian or Asian-American (10.6%), Hispanic/Latino/Mexican-American (5.7%), and Black or African-American (3.0%). By school year, 36.7% of participants were freshmen, 44.3% sophomores, 11.7% juniors, and 7.2% seniors. Just 13.9% of the sample identified as LGBTQ.

Measures

Social desirability was assessed with the Marlowe-Crown Social Desirability Scale (MC SDS; Marlowe & Crowne, 1960), a 33-item true/false measure of a respondent's need for social approval. A representative item is, "I have never intensely disliked anyone." Evidence for convergent and discriminant validity has been reported (Marlowe & Crowne, 1961). Higher scores reflect a greater motivation to present oneself in a manner consistent with perceived cultural and social expectations.

Perceived campus climate was assessed with 15 self-report items developed by Elze (2003) based on focus groups with adolescents who identified as lesbian, gay, or bisexual. These items were used to measure 10 positive and 5 negative characteristics of the campus environment. Sample positive characteristics include "Faculty members care about gay/lesbian/bisexual students," and "Guest speakers come to campus to discuss issues important to gay/lesbian/bisexual students." Sample negative characteristics include "Gay/lesbian/bisexual students experience verbal abuse on campus," and "Faculty members on campus tell gay jokes." The scale author reported factor analytic evidence for positive and negative characteristics as separate dimensions as well as evidence for internal consistency with a high school population (α = .84 for positive, α = .70 for negative). In the current study, these items were assessed on a 4-point scale (0 = *not at all*, 3 = *a lot*). Items within each subscale were summed so that higher scores reflected more of each type of characteristics of the campus climate. Compared to the high school students interviewed by Elze, college students who identify as LGBTQ describe experiencing similar negative campus characteristics and report appreciating similar positive characteristics (e.g., Phoenix, 2011; Rankin, 2003; Tetreault, Fette, Meidlinger, & Hope, 2013; University of North Florida, 2011). In the current sample, the estimates of internal consistency were acceptable for positive (Cronbach's α = .78) and negative (Cronbach's α = .78) characteristics.

Participants' sexual orientation and gender identity each were assessed with a single item. Participants' sexual orientation was queried with the open-ended question, "How would you describe your sexual orientation?" Gender identity was queried by asking participants to circle all that apply: "male," "female," "trans," "cis," and "other." In response to the open-ended question, LGBTQ students self-identified in various ways, including "bicurious," "bi/demi," "bisexual," "gay," "homosexual," "lesbian," "pansexual," "polysexual," "questioning," and "trans lesbian." Non-LGBTQ students were classified on the basis of identifying as heterosexual and not identifying as transgender, for example "straight," "heterosexual," or "cisgender heterosexual." Three participants who identified as "asexual" and three participants who did not respond to the items about sexual orientation and gender identity could not be classified as either LGBTQ or non-LGBTQ.

Procedure

Undergraduate students were recruited through a voluntary human participant pool for an anonymous study of "Attitudes about Different Kinds of People and our Campus Community." Data collection sessions were held in classrooms and lasted no more than one hour. All participants were seated in alternating rows to ensure privacy. After providing informed consent, participants were randomly assigned to receive a packet of measures with an excerpt of a fictitious syllabus that either did or did not include a Safe Zone symbol (appended). Participants responded to self-report measures of social desirability and traditional and modern homophobia, were asked to read and answer questions about a fictitious syllabus excerpt, and then responded to measures of perceived campus climate. After completing these measures, participants submitted study materials face down into a folder for privacy and were fully debriefed. Participants earned course credit for their time. All study procedures were approved by the Institutional Review Board.

RESULTS

About 53.7% (*n* = 138) of participants were randomly assigned to the Safe Zone symbol condition, whereas 46.3% (*n* = 120) were assigned to the control condition. Univariate analyses suggested that random assignment produced comparable groups. That is, those assigned to the symbol condition did not significantly differ from those in the control condition with regard to age, race/ethnicity, class year, gender, or LGBTQ status. Furthermore, participants did not significantly differ in self-reported social desirability scores. Across conditions, participants perceived many positive characteristics of the campus climate for LGBTQ students ($M = 20.14$, $SD = 5.15$, observed range 7 to 30, possible range 0 to 30) and they perceived few negative characteristics ($M = 1.88$, $SD = 2.01$, observed range 0 to 11, possible range 0 to 15).

The primary study hypothesis was that students randomly assigned to view a Safe Zone symbol would report more favorable perceptions of the campus climate than control students who were randomly assigned not to view a Safe Zone symbol. To test this hypothesis, a single factor multivariate analysis of variance (MANOVA) was conducted with positive and negative characteristics of the campus climate as dependent variables. The overall analysis was significant, $F(2, 261) = 3.28$, $p < .05$, Wilks' Lambda = .98.

Univariate follow-up analyses revealed a significant main effect of exposure to the Safe Zone symbol on perceived positive characteristics of the campus climate, $F(1, 262) = 5.61$, $p < .05$. That is, students who viewed the Safe Zone symbol reported perceiving more positive characteristics ($M = 20.83$, $SD = 4.99$) than students who did not ($M = 19.33$, $SD = 5.24$). In contrast, exposure to the Safe Zone symbol was not associated with differences in perceived negative characteristics of the campus climate, $F(1, 262) < 1$, $p = .37$.

DISCUSSION

The present study evaluated the effect of brief exposure to a Safe Zone symbol on college students' perceptions of campus climate characteristics affecting LGBTQ students. Students were randomly assigned to conditions in which they viewed a fictitious syllabus extract that either did or did not feature a Safe Zone symbol. As expected, students who were exposed to the Safe Zone symbol perceived more positive campus climate characteristics for LGBTQ students.

This favorable result adds to a growing body of ethnographic, qualitative, and correlational studies documenting the favorable effects of Safe Zone and related programs on campus communities (e.g., Evans, 2002; Ratts et al., 2013, Szalacha, 2003). The current results expand on past observational studies by adding experimental evidence for the beneficial effect of even a brief exposure to a single Safe Zone symbol on perceived climate. The current study also informs a previously unknown relationship between Safe Zone programs and existing climate on campuses. More specifically, it was unclear from existing research whether implementing a Safe Zone program improves campus climate, whether campuses with more accepting climates were more likely to implement Safe Zone initiatives in the first place, or both. The current study begins to address this gap by showing that exposure to a Safe Zone symbol affects perceptions of campus climate for LGBTQ students. Additional research is needed to examine the effect of exposure to Safe Zone symbols on actual campus climate, including community members' attitudes about LGBTQ students. To our knowledge, however, this study offers the first experimental evidence demonstrating the positive impact of the Safe Zone symbol, the most visible aspect of the Safe Zone program, on perceptions of the campus climate.

The current study also extends existing research demonstrating the important role of symbols and imagery in shaping attitudes and behavior. More specifically, in past research, brief exposure to images associated with schools (such as lockers, classrooms) led to support for school taxes (Berger et al., 2008) and brief exposure to the American flag led to more conservative beliefs, attitudes, and voting behavior (Carter et al., 2011). The current study expands upon these past studies by focusing on the perceptions of general attitudes of others in the community toward a specific population: LGBTQ students. Of note, in past research, such symbols have been studied as "primes" (Berger et al., p. 8848), "incidental cues" (Carter et al., 2011, p. 1014), or both. This may also be true of the Safe Zone symbols displayed in the experimental condition of the current study. However, Safe Zone symbols are intended to be more than incidental cues or primes: they are displayed in an explicit attempt to communicate acceptance of LGBTQ individuals and inclusive attitudes more generally (e.g., Ratts et al., 2013).

Future research is also needed to identify additional potential effects of exposure to a Safe Zone symbol. In the current study, exposure to a Safe Zone symbol was associated with perceptions of more positive but not more negative characteristics of the campus climate for LGBTQ students. One possible explanation for this pattern of findings is that perceptions of negative characteristics were quite low. However, it might also be speculated that the presence of a positive cue, a Safe Zone symbol, impacts perceived positive characteristics of the campus climate (like the presence of supportive allies) more so than negative ones (like others' use of homophobic slurs). Additional research should examine other potential effects of exposure to a Safe Zone symbol on other outcomes, such as both explicit and implicit attitudes about people who are LGBTQ and behavior toward those who are perceived to be LGBTQ. For example, Ferguson and Hassin (2007) found brief exposure to the American flag increased aggressive thoughts and behavior. If the same type of pattern extends to brief exposure to a Safe Zone symbol, exposure to a Safe Zone symbol could promote more prosocial thoughts and behavior, both in general or perhaps specifically in response to microaggressions like "that's so gay" (Woodford, Howell, Kulick, & Silverschanz, 2013). Future research is also needed to examine the durability of the effect of viewing a Safe Zone symbol on perceptions of campus climate.

The current research suggests that campuses without active Safe Zone programs may benefit from implementing such programs. That is, the visible symbol of the program has a measurably positive impact on perceptions of the campus climate. More generally, the current research implies that core values of many colleges, as expressed by student affairs professional organizations, can be at least partly addressed through Safe Zone programs and symbols. For example, according to the website of the college where the study took place, guiding principles for the campus community include integrity, innovation, and diversity. Implementing Safe Zone programs and associ-

ated policies aligns with these values, and displaying the Safe Zone symbol is one way to quickly, effectively communicate that the campus adheres to these principles.

The current research also suggests that campuses that already have active Safe Zone programs and policies would likely benefit from directing student attention to the Safe Zone symbol along with sharing information about Safe Zone programs and policies. Multiple examples of such practices could be used throughout students' time on campus. For example, an orientation program might introduce the Safe Zone program and associated symbol to the group and invite new students to count how many symbols they can find on campus. These introductory comments could then be used to segue into more meaningful conversations such as group dialogues that promote "intergroup understanding, intergroup collaboration and action, and relevancy of diversity in higher education" (Thakral et al., 2015, p. 1). Furthermore, faculty and staff who are Safe Zone trained might also include the symbol in multiple places, such as class syllabi as well as office doors and announcements for speakers. Doing so might highlight for students that faculty members are open to diverse points of view, which in turn, positively predicts students' own openness to diversity (Ryder, Reason, Mitchell, Gillon, & Hemer, 2015).

To our knowledge, the current study is the first to report experimental evidence for the benefit of exposure to Safe Zone symbols on perceived campus climate. Overall, results suggested that those who viewed a Safe Zone symbol reported a more positive perception of the campus climate. Additional research on the impact of initiatives to support LGBTQ students is needed to provide an inclusive learning environment—not merely the perception of an inclusive environment—for all students.

APPENDIX

All participants viewed the following fictitious syllabus excerpt. Those in the experimental condition viewed the excerpt below with the Safe Zone symbol. Those in the control condition viewed the excerpt below without the Safe Zone symbol.

****

Group Conflict

Instructor: Dr. X

Dept: Sociology

Office: Bailey 013

Email: x@schoolname.edu

In this class, we will be both studying and experiencing group dynamics and group conflict. In addition to traditional readings and lectures about stages of group development, you'll spend time in groups exploring various identity categories and continuums (e.g., gender). Group members will explore patterns of similarity and differences within each group, and then later, group members will work with other formed groups to learn more about the unique experiences of others. More generally, you'll be expected to integrate knowledge about group dynamics to analyze your work both within your group and between different groups. In addition, you will be asked to make a communication profile for yourself, indicating your perceived strengths and weaknesses, and to keep a communications journal that tracks your achievements, challenges, and progress. I'll be available to meet with individuals and groups to help resolve any difficult issues that may arise, and I'm dedicated to helping provide an inclusive class community and environment.

REFERENCES

Berger, J., Meredith, M., & Wheeler, S. C. (2008). Contextual priming: Where people vote affects how they vote. *Proceedings of the National Academy of Sciences of the United States of America, 105*(26), 8846-8849. doi:10.1073/pnas.0711988105

Black, W. W., Fedewa, A. L., & Gonzalez, K. A. (2012). Effects of "safe school" programs and policies on the social climate for sexual-minority youth: A review of the literature. *Journal of LGBT Youth, 9*(4), 321-339. doi:10.1080/1936 1653.2012.714343

Brown, R. D., Clarke, B., Gortmaker, V., & Robinson-Keilig, R. (2004). Assessing the campus climate for gay, lesbian, bisexual, and transgender (GLBT) students using a multiple perspectives approach. *Journal of College Student Development, 45*(1), 8-26. doi:10.1353/csd.2004.0003

Carter, T. J., Ferguson, M. J., & Hassin, R. R. (2011). A single exposure to the American flag shifts support toward Republicanism up to 8 months later. *Psychological Science, 22*(8), 1011-1018. doi:10.1177/0956797611414726

Elze, D. E. (2003). Gay, lesbian, and bisexual youths' perceptions of their high school environments and comfort in school. *Children & Schools, 25*(4), 225-239. doi:10.1093/cs/25.4.225

Evans, N. J. (2002). The impact of an LGBT safe zone project on campus climate. *Journal of College Student Development, 43*(4), 522-539.

Ferguson, M. J., & Hassin, R. R. (2007). On the automatic association between America and aggression for news watchers. *Personality and Social Psychology Bulletin, 33*(12), 1632-1647. doi:10.1177/0146167207307493

Finkel, M. J., Storaasli, R. D., Bandele, A., & Schaefer, V. (2003). Diversity training in graduate school: An exploratory evaluation of the Safe Zone project. *Professional Psychology: Research and Practice, 34*(5), 555-561. doi:10.1037/0735-7028.34.5.555

Hassin, R. R., Ferguson, M. J., Shidlovski, D., & Gross, T. (2007). Subliminal exposure to national flags affects political thought and behavior. *Proceedings of the National Academy of Sciences of the United States of America, 104*(50), 19757-19761. doi:10.1073/pnas.0704679104

Kosciw, J. G., Greytak, E. A., Palmer, N. A., & Boesen, M. J. (2014). *The 2013 National School Survey: The experiences of lesbian, gay, bisexual, and transgender youth in our nation's schools.* New York, NY: GLSEN. Retrieved from http://www.glsen.org/article/2013-national-school-climate-survey

Marlowe, D., & Crowne, D. P. (1960). A new scale of social desirability independent of psychopathology. *Journal of Consulting Psychology, 24*(4), 349-354. doi:10.1037/h0047358

Marlowe, D., & Crowne, D. P. (1961). Social desirability and response to situational demands. *Journal of Consulting Psychology, 25*(2), 109-115. doi:10.1037/h0041627

Phoenix, T. L. (2011). *Campus climate regarding sexual orientation, gender identity, and gender expression: A report issued by the provost's committee on LGBT life.* Unpublished manuscript, University of North Carolina at Chapel Hill. Retrieved from http://provost.unc.edu/files/2012/09/campusclimatereport.pdf

Rankin, S. R. (2003). *Campus climate for gay, lesbian, bisexual, and transgender people: A national perspective.* New York, NY: The Policy Institute of the National Gay and Lesbian Task Force. Retrieved from http://www.thetaskforce.org/static_html/downloads/reports/reports/CampusClimate.pdf

Ratts, M. J., Kaloper, M., McReady, C., Tighe, L., Butler, S. K., Dempsey, K., & McCullough, J. (2013). Safe space programs in K-12 schools: Creating a visible presence of LGBTQ allies. *Journal of LGBT Issues in Counseling, 7*(4), 387-404. doi:10.1080/15538605.2013.839344

Ryder, A. J., Reason, R. D., Mitchell, J. J., Gillon, K., & Hemer, K. M. (2015). Climate for learning and students' openness to diversity and challenge: A critical role for faculty. *Journal of Diversity in Higher Education, 9*(4), 339-352. doi:10.1037/a0039766

Szalacha, L. A. (2003). Safe sexual diversity climates: Lessons learned from an evaluation of Massachusetts safe school program for gay and lesbian students. *American Journal of Education, 110*(1), 58-88. doi:10.1086/377673

Tetreault, P. A., Fette, R., Meidlinger, P. C., & Hope, D. (2013). Perceptions of campus climate by sexual minorities. *Journal of Homosexuality, 60*(7), 947-964. doi:10.1080/00918369.2013.7 74874 0.1080/00918369.2013.774874

Thakral, C., Vasquez, P. L., Bottoms, B. L., Matthews, A. K., Hudson, K. M., & Whitley, S. K. (2015). Understanding difference through dialogue: A first-year experience for college students. *Journal of Diversity in Higher Education, 9*(2), 130-142. doi:10.1037/a0039935

University of North Florida Commission on Diversity, & Committee on Lesbian, Gay, Bisexual and Transgender Equity. (2011). *University of North Florida campus climate for sexual orientation and gender identity and expression.* Unpublished manuscript, University of North Florida. Retrieved from https://www.unf.edu/uploadedFiles/sa/lgbt/CampusClimateJune2011.pdf

Woodford, M. R. Howell, M. L., Kulick, A., & Silverschanz, P. (2013). That's so gay: Heterosexual male undergraduates and the perpetuation of sexual orientation microaggressions on campus. *Journal of Interpersonal Violence, 28*(2), 416-435. doi:10.1177/0886260512454719

Yost, M. R., & Gilmore, S. (2011). Assessing LGBTQ campus climate and creating change. *Journal of Homosexuality, 58*(9), 1330-1354. doi:10.1080/00918369.2011.605744

A Reflection with Brendan Mahoney, *The Proceedings of GREAT Day* Editor

What's great for you about GREAT Day?

Mahoney: GREAT Day is an excellent day to just enjoy what this school community is capable of doing. For us as editors of this journal, though, there's an added excitement of seeing what might potentially appear in our issue next year. As we walk from presentation to presentation on this day meant to celebrate Geneseo's achievement, we're acutely aware of how far this achievement can go. Every year we're lucky enough to publish some of Geneseo's most innovative academic and creative work, and GREAT Day is the very first look we get into which innovative works we get to publish next year.

What impact do you think GREAT Day has on our campus culture?

Mahoney: The answer that comes to mind first, as we are an academic institution, is simply that it adds an awareness or emphasis on academic excellence, but it's important to remember that neither Geneseo nor GREAT Day only celebrates academic work. There are plenty of students at this school training for skills that reach far beyond academia. GREAT Day allows for a celebration of those skills in addition to purely academic ones. GREAT Day's effect on campus culture, therefore, should not be thought of so narrowly as emphasizing academic achievement. Rather, it emphasizes all achievement and ensures the students of Geneseo that, no matter what they're currently studying, they have a space to showcase any and all of their skills.

Why does undergraduate research in general matter to you?

Mahoney: Selfishly, undergraduate research matters to us very much as it's what allows us to produce this wonderful journal every year. But, more generally, undergraduate research gives plenty of young academics the opportunity to think creatively. Rather than being enlisted to do the grunt calculations on a math problem or to collect 400 sources for some graduate student's dissertation, Geneseo's focus on undergraduate research allows its students to challenge themselves and grow as researchers by expecting them to set their own goals and pursue them largely on their own. This allows Geneseo to produce the kinds of graduates who leave with a sense of confidence and go on in their careers to accomplish things that make us proud of publishing their work.

What's your interest in the specific topic being researched in the following paper?

Mahoney: Our interest at the time of accepting this piece was obvious; the relationship between the American media and Middle Eastern conflict has long been criticized as a warped and biased one. Recently, our interest has become more prescient than ever. There is a very real need for clear and unbiased communication between the American public and the people of the Middle East, or else there is a very real chance that people will die. Foreign policy decisions cannot be made based on the narratives woven by television personalities, and Katherine's work in dissecting those narratives is valuable.

Kill or Be Killed: Seeing the Middle East as a Threat to the Western World

Katherine Zaslavsky

ABSTRACT

In the context of Middle Eastern conflict, fear is a powerful tool that can sway Western opinion for or against certain causes, as seen through the use of framing. Even outside of fear's overt usage in the media, narratives tend to separate the West from the Middle East. The presence of these narratives, and the extent of this presence, is indicative of increasingly divisive relations between the West and the Middle East, driven by fear of alien peoples. This research identified, defined, and analyzed the frames used in American broadcast television coverage of the Arab–Israeli conflict and Islamic acts of terrorism. It established the textual makeup of independent narratives, which will allow for more involved macroanalysis of framing relationships.

Western civilization has long viewed the Middle East as an exotic land, "set[ting] up boundaries between their land and its immediate surroundings and the territories beyond, which they call 'the land of the barbarians'" (Said, 1979, p. 54). It is through this lens of the media that such views are exacerbated and perpetuated during times of crisis. Many of these divisions and their justifications are based on long-held fabrications of the Orient, especially the Middle East and the Islamic people who reside there (Said, 1979). Even the advent of modern mass media, with their ability to transmit information across geographical boundaries, has not succeeded in clarifying vague, inaccurate views of the Middle East and Islam (Said, 1997, p. 5). In fact, in light of contemporary events, Said (1997) states:

> Overtly Muslim countries like Iran threaten "us" [the West] and our way of life, and speculations about the latest conspiracy to blow up buildings, sabotage commercial airliners, and poison water supplies seem to play increasingly on the Western consciousness. (p. xi)

The urgency of such claims and their implications, such as the allocation of military resources in the Middle East and the breakdown of relations between countries in a global economy, deem it necessary to examine the verity of such claims and to present an accurate view of the Middle East and the people who live there. This collective growth of knowledge can invaluably foster stronger, safer relations between the West and the Middle East.

LITERATURE REVIEW

Media Framing

This study seeks to examine the framing, especially through language, used in American media coverage of violent events related to the Middle East—specifically, those occurring within the Arab–Israeli conflict and those that have been characterized as Islamic terrorist acts. Framing, as defined by Entman (2004), is the process of "selecting and highlighting some facets of events or issues, and making connections among them so as to promote a particular interpretation, evaluation, and/or solution" (p. 5). Entman identifies the cascade activation model as the specific medium through which the official views of the government become the legitimized views of the hegemony. Because frames pervade government agencies by affecting policy and resource allocation as well as the public consciousness, their definitions are significant both symbolically and literally (Gitlin, 1980). Furthermore, frames are naturally reproduced throughout the media: "The more often journalists hear similar thoughts expressed by their sources and by other news outlets, the more likely their own thoughts will run along those lines" (Entman, 2004, p. 9). For this reason, it is necessary to define and assess significant frames and their interconnectivity as independent variables, as well as their relation to audiences who are learning to understand unfamiliar geographic areas and events.

Using Media Frames to Characterize the Middle East

With regard to conflict in unfamiliar areas, such as Israel and the recently recognized state of Palestine, frames affect American audience's perceptions and their investment in the conflict (Sheafer & Dvir-Gvirsman, 2010). The ways by which Western media relate these issues to their audiences define the reactions of those audiences and their support of and investment in the future actions of Western governments, according to Entman's (2004) cascade activation model. Therefore, language alluding to conflict and the conditions thereof is especially important among media schema, as it determines the relation between the audience and foreign cultures.

The cultural divisions between West and non-West (in this case, the United States and the Middle East) are clear enough in their abstract presence, but their manifestations in sources of information such as media extend beyond the abstract to influence Western views on global policy and relations to Middle Eastern states (Chomsky, 2007). Public support for Western global policy, then, becomes a commodity that can be affected by and controlled through media frames; it attains a new level of significance in determining public support of and perceived worth of relevant governmental agencies (Nacos, 2002; Nacos, Bloch-Elkon, & Shapiro, 2011). Interactions between constituents and policy makers take place largely in the realm of media. These constituents observe and assess their representatives who then gauge their constituents' views in order to maintain their bases of support (Entman, 2004). Therefore, when the media portray a third group of people from an area outside the relevant political jurisdiction, this group is not directly involved in its own representation and interpretation, and both constituents and politicians form their views on the sole basis of the media coverage.

In such instances, frames transcend their symbolic roles as lenses through which to view a particular topic that one might encounter in some form of reality (Altheide, 1997). They become the reality for media audiences who do not look further into the events being portrayed, and they naturally use these views, the truth as they know it, to form opinions and to decide American global policy (e.g., Altheide, 1997; Entman, 2004). In the cases of the Arab–Israeli conflict and Islamic acts of terrorism, extreme violence and accounts of definite blame are the reality for Western audiences. Without truly exhaustive analytical reporting, the United States views "the Middle East as a spectacle about which one was supposed to be excited" (Said, 1992, p. 183), a separate and alien zone of violence. Therefore, acts of Islamic terrorism against the West are frightening not only in their form of brutality and violence, but also in their capacity to cause the spread of this violence to other areas and harm those who are alien to the original conflict (Nacos, 2002; Nacos, 2007). The juxtaposition of a safe Western world being exposed to the violence of the turbulent Middle East results in a specific, evocative state: fear.

Fear as a Political Weapon

The Western media have played a significant role in establishing the dichotomy of safety versus danger in terms of the threats that people fear (Glassner, 1999). The media are a primary avenue through which moral panics spread, allowing audiences to learn of the threats to their well-being and the ways by which they can protect themselves from these threats (Gerbner & Morgan, 2002; Hunt, 1997). In standard examples of moral panics, the threat typically originates from within some section of society as opposed to a section outside the bounds of the given society, and it is therefore presented as a domestic issue (Hunt, 1997).

However, in the cases considered in this study, the threat being constructed is an outside force on a massive scale, that of the entire Middle Eastern people (Nacos & Torres-Reyna, 2007; Said, 1997). For centuries, the overwhelming majority of Western impressions of the Middle East have reflected feelings of superiority, disdain, and even disgust; however, there has been a trend toward media coverage focusing on the inherently dangerous and barbaric nature of Middle Easterners as a people whose existence threatens the peace of the West (Said, 1979; Said, 1997). In addition, Altheide's (1997) identification of fear as a "*vocabulary of motive*—certain characteristics and identities are attributed to those persons we associate with fearing acts" (p. 663)—designates the language of fear as the language of blame. Due to ambivalent characterization in the news, actors in these situations, specifically Middle Easterners, become associated with acts of violence that were committed by those of their ethnicity (Gerbner, Mowlana, & Schiller, 1996; Said, 1997).

Gerbner (1980) and Glassner (1999) assert that sensationalism is rewarded in media, motivating newsmakers to focus on stories of violence and horror. Therefore, it is not surprising that Western audiences are so overwhelmingly exposed to negative views of the Middle East (Said, 1997). Furthermore, agencies, politicians, and activists whose funding and support rely on public opinion are also able to appeal to audiences by drawing on reports that evoke fear in order to highlight the value of their causes (Gerbner, 1977; Glassner, 1999). In the case of terrorism, Malhotra and Popp (2012) found "reducing perceived threat substantially decreases support for policies intended to combat terrorism" (p. 34). This directly affects support for and funding of a counterterrorism agency, which makes the threat of attack an economic commodity that can result in increased support and funding for that agency (Chomsky, 2007; Eytan, 2002; Nacos et al., 2011; Savun & Philips, 2009).

Certain audiences are particularly susceptible to fear stimuli in the media. Hatemi, McDermott, Eaves, Kendler, and Neale (2013) found that genetically influenced personal traits, such as social phobia, are related to negative attitudes toward out-groups, such as people whose social conditions and attributes differ from those of the subjects. Fear of Middle Easterners as a cultural and geographical out-group can be targeted at certain audiences to elicit the most powerful and effective responses at both the individual and the societal levels (Gerbner, 1988; Glassner, 1999). Through the problem frame described by Altheide (1997), media purport to link a certain issue or problem to a certain solution, playing on "the audience's familiarity with narratives that spell out simple and clear truths" (p. 655), such as the dichotomy between evil and good. This is essentially an extension on moral panics, linking the moral issue to the interests of those who purportedly provide a solution (Altheide, 1997).

Media Coverage of Islamic Terrorism and the Arab–Israeli Conflict

This dichotomy, as well as its implications for American foreign policy, was never so relevant as it is in the current "crisis" of Islamic terrorism, in the wake of such widely publicized and far-reaching events as 9/11 and the increasingly tumultuous relationship between the United States and Iran (Nacos, 1994; Nacos et al., 2011; Said, 1997). Terrorism is a threat perceived throughout all major social institutions in the United States, pervading American culture and saturating it with images and phrases that characterize Middle Easterners as inherently violent beings, their views antithetical to those held by democratic powers (Nacos, 1994, 2002). Acts of Islamic terrorism are seen as unjustifiable, despite viewers' lack of knowledge of pertinent social conditions, especially when contrasted with the self-legitimized actions of Western counterterrorism operatives in the Middle East (Chomsky, 2007; Kruglanski & Fishman, 2006). It is essentially a moral panic, in which most Americans are unclear on the extent of their actual risk but are willing to support public policy that claims to protect them; they "buy" the fear that the media advertise to them, despite the reality of terrorist attacks (e.g., Chomsky, 2007; Enders & Sandler, 1999; Nacos et al., 2011; Norris, Kern, & Just, 2003). This directly affects policy changes and the population's investment in overseas military action, as well as the United States' relations with the Middle East, all while keeping public attention on horrendous acts of terrorism and the perpetrators of those acts (Gilboa, 2002; Wolfsfeld, 1997).

Even the Arab–Israeli conflict, which is distanced both politically and geographically from the United States, is susceptible to such perceptions by American viewers. American media identify with the Israeli cause and portray Palestinians as aggressors within the frame of the violent Middle East, adhering to their "inherently violent" nature (Chomsky, 2003; Chomsky, 2007; Suleiman, 1974). This viewpoint has long been the official stand of the American government and the hegemonic frame in American media coverage of the Arab–Israeli conflict (Chomsky, 2007; Gilboa, 1987; Suleiman, 1974). Because the United States views Israel as a democratic political ally, American media frame this as a civil conflict, in which terrorist rebels (displaced Palestinians) are aggressing against Israel (Bizman & Hoffman, 1993; Chomsky, 2007; Said, 1992; Savun & Philips, 2009). Portrayed as a legitimate state within this frame, Israel has full justification to defend itself against the unwarranted attacks of Palestinians (Chomsky, 2003; Chomsky, 2007). However, in recent decades there has arisen a competing (although not hegemonic) frame: that of Palestinians victimized by Israelis, civilians who are unnecessarily targeted by Israeli defense operations (Gilboa, 1987; Wolfsfeld, 1997).

Past research on media coverage of the Arab–Israeli conflict and acts of terrorism shows unifying elements in the frames used to cover both types of events (Chomsky, 2007; Wolfsfeld, 1997; Wolfsfeld, 2004). However, no formal analysis has been undertaken to determine the exact makeup of these frames and the extent to which they are present in American media. Given the political, governmental, military, and cultural value of those viewpoints and the lives that are affected or terminated based on their ramifications, it is crucial to ascertain the truth behind the frames (e.g., Haklai, 2009; Wolfsfeld, 2004).

METHODS

Sample

This study analyzes American media coverage of the Arab–Israeli conflict and of Islamic acts of terrorism in order to determine trends in the frames used. While these events are not representative of all violence linked to the Middle East, they are significant examples of such violence (e.g., Nacos et al., 2011; Wolfsfeld, 2004). In particular, it focuses on the medium of broadcast television, Americans' most popular source of news (Saad, 2013). Analysis is limited to the language used in covering the Arab–Israeli conflict and Islamic terrorism, as language is a primary indicator of problem frames, to which specific terms can be linked (Altheide, 1997; Hunt, 1997). This sample consists of relevant transcripts of ABC, CBS, and NBC newscasts, accessed through the *LexisNexis* database. These networks have the highest levels of viewership and salience among Americans (e.g., Behr & Iyengar, 1985; Guskin, Jurkowitz, & Mitchell, 2013; Meadow, 1972; Olmstead, Jurkowitz, Mitchell, & Enda, 2013). Because of their popularity and reputation for (relative) reliability, the frames portrayed by these networks reflect the frames

to which most television viewers are exposed. Analyzing transcripts from these sources therefore draws on the data that are most relevant to and reflective of the experiences of the general public, especially given the rise of publicized Islamic terrorist groups, such as ISIS, and the increasing political turbulence within and around the Middle East (e.g., Bayat, 2015; "Iraq profile," 2015; "Timeline," 2014). Given the timeframes of these events, transcripts were selected only from the period 2010-2014 in order to capture those events which were relevant and had not been covered in previous literature.

Identification and Categorization of Narratives

The analysis utilized in this study employs both qualitative and quantitative methods. The qualitative procedure consists of examining a sample of approximately 5% of 2,348 total transcripts, recording the subject matter and the language used in reporting the acts of violence. All terms present in the transcripts are organized into narrative categorizies (also referred to as "frames") based on their definitions and the context in which they were typically used within coverage of the relevant events, drawing on the combination of qualitative analysis and a computer program designed by a faculty member of the university where this study takes place. The program identifies all unique terms present in every transcript, as well as their frequencies, then parses through every transcript by sentence, identifying each occurrence of a term from a given category. The results are a complete record of the frequency of occurrences of each category throughout the transcripts, which allows for analysis and ease of identifying trends among the frames. For efficient analysis, these categories are mutually exclusive, outside the frames of *Palestine* and *Israel*, which separate the terms from "Arab–Israeli Conflict" into terms that referred to Palestine and those that referred to Israel (see Table 1).

The final step of qualitative analysis consisted of in-depth textual analysis of two transcripts, selected on the basis of their representative nature. The first is "Middle East on the brink: Rain of fire," cast on ABC (Sawyer & Marquadt, 2012). This story was selected because it presents accounts of violence enacted on both the Palestinian and the Israeli sides of the Arab–Israeli conflict. These acts are presented within the context of ongoing violence, rather than as a result of a single specific act that brought unusual attention to the area. The language used in this transcript therefore addresses the conditions of that violence within the same segment, allowing for clear comparison of the language used to address the two sides. The second transcript is an account of a terror threat, a prime example of the many times when fear of violence brought coverage to terrorism (Schieffer et al., 2013). Audiences depend on news media to warn them of impending danger, and in such cases the media present the background on these possible threats. Similar to the ongoing conflict between Palestine and Israel, these threats represent an ongoing state of violence that is in danger of bleeding into the United States through terrorist attacks. This account of one such threat is therefore representative of the majority of the transcripts that cover Islamic terrorism.

ANALYSIS

Defining the Narratives

It is through the use of common narratives in media that one is able to assess the utilized frameworks within these conflicts. The results of this research show strong presences of similarities between coverage of the Arab–Israeli conflict and that of acts of Islamic terrorism. For example, the *VictimCasualties* frame is indicative of a report that focuses on the casualties of an act of violence as opposed to the perpetrators of that act (*BlameIncarceration*). Narratives such as *Terror*, *VictimCasualties*, *Warzone*, *Violence*, *IllegitimateState*, and *Protest* present the Middle East as an unstable geographic area, the setting of ongoing conflict and destitution, which disqualifies it as a political actor equal to the United States (see Table 2). By contrast, the *LegitimateState*, *Defense*, and *Honor* narratives serve to define the United States and their actions as legitimate and justifiable, understandable in the eyes of the audience (see Table 2).

Narratives that address the framing of acts of violence are *Terror*, *Warzone*, *Defense*, *ResponseRevenge*, *BlameIncarceration*, *Honor*, and *Threat* (see Table 2). The distinctions between these define the audience's perception of acts of violence. The *Warzone* narrative defines the violence as ongoing, occurring in an acceptable format, such as war. *Defense*, *ResponseRevenge*, and *Honor* are narratives that provide justi-

fication for the violence being addressed, presenting the act as legitimate in its capacity to protect a people (see Table 2). They shift blame away from the perpetrators, all the while acknowledging their actions, formulating conditions that favor the perpetrators from the audience's viewpoint. The *Honor* narrative goes even further to present the perpetrators in a noble light, while the *BlameIncarceration* frame serves the opposite purpose, alienating the audience from the perpetrators and designating them as deviants. The *Threat* narrative has its own connotations, as the words that fall into this category address the possibility of violence, maintaining its relevance to audiences that are physically separate from the conflict. These designations are often subtle, but they effectually design a spectrum of assigned guilt on which perpetrators are placed, defining a viewer's understanding of the event and the people involved.

Terms used to identify the audience with victims are included under *VictimCasualties*, *Warzone*, and *FearSorrowRage*—these narratives establish specific persons as victims of their surroundings (even when they are committing acts of violence), thereby aligning audiences with their sentiments. *ResolutionSafety* and *Recovery* narratives are extensions on this concept, dealing with the aftermath of the violence, again with tendencies to sympathize with the victims of violence. As the roles of perpetrator and victim are easily interchangeable in situations of ongoing violence, media usage of specific narratives designating these labels to specific sides is essential to establishing the audience's interpretation of the event.

The remaining narratives (*ArabIsraeli*, *Palestine*, *Israel*, *USWesternWorld*, *Religion*, and *IslamMiddleEast*) are identifiers of specific entities. Further application of quantitative methods will allow for analysis of the ways in which other narratives are used relative to these identifiers, beyond the qualitative observations present in this study.

Arab–Israeli Conflict

A classic example of this portrayal of turmoil in the context of the Arab–Israeli conflict is the segment "Middle East on the brink; rain of fire," cast on ABC (Sawyer & Marquadt, 2012). This piece introduces "the holy city of Jerusalem, under fire" (Sawyer & Marquadt, 2012, para. 3), a juxtaposition of innocence against an onslaught of violence. Jerusalem is identified as a religious place, a sanctuary that would not be involved in the violence were it not being targeted; this is a clear utilization of the *Religion* narrative in the process of advancing the portrayed innocence of the victims. "Under fire" is a manifestation of the *Violence* narrative, and it inherently assigns blame by its presence, informing the audience that not only is a religious sanctuary involved in violence, it is the victim of an attack. The reporter of this article then mentions "families huddled in concrete pipes for safety" (Sawyer & Marquadt, 2012, para. 5), an elaboration on Jerusalem's state of victimhood and that of its citizens. They are punished for their geographic position, forced to pay with the risk of injury or death.

Presenting these subjects as "families," as opposed to "people," is an example of the use of the *VictimCasualties* frame. It elevates their perceived innocence by stating that they are not isolated individuals but are emotionally connected human beings with whom the audience can connect. Again, the use of the *VictimCasualties* frame has the dual effect of presenting a specific subject as innocent and relatable to the audience, to an attempt to evoke the sympathy from viewers. In this excerpt, "safety" is a manifestation of the *ResolutionSafety* narrative, representing a possible end to the violence. It heightens the desperation of these families' situations, suggesting that their fear of danger and their need for safety is so great that they must huddle in pipes to survive. In the context of a warzone, the *ResolutionSafety* narrative presents American audiences a victimized people that emphasizes the disparity between their safety and the dangerous conditions under which the subjects live.

This effect is a defining force behind the statements of the reporter, including such lines as "no letup in this deadly escalation" (Sawyer & Marquadt, 2012, para. 10), another phrase used to describe the plight of the Israelis. "Escalation" is an example of the *Warzone* narrative, implying that there is an ongoing conflict occurring, in which this particular event is a temporary swell. However, this is contrasted with the term "no letup," which implies that what ought to be a temporary swell is lasting longer than expected; because this is an act of violence, extending it becomes extreme violence, an escalation that inflames the audience. "Letup" belongs to the *ResolutionSafety*

frame, and its negation is another portrayal of desperation, highlighting the constant danger that will not allow citizens the luxury of safety enjoyed by the audience. Furthermore, "deadly" is a term from the *Violence* narrative, a word that is inherently linked to life-threatening violence. Even without further elaboration, "deadly" describes a situation of extreme danger, which, in conjunction with "no letup," inflames the audience with its portrayal of these victimized people.

Similar language is used in portraying the Palestinian side of the conflict, as the reporter states that there has been "almost no letup in the Israeli warplanes hammering of Gaza" (Sawyer & Marquadt, 2012, para. 27). Again, "no letup" functions in the same way to present the people as victims of an ongoing conflict, innocent bystanders in an environment engulfed in violence. However, this statement follows the description of the Israeli victims, as well as the reporter's statement that Palestinian militants were launching rockets at Israel, victimizing its citizens as aforementioned. In addition, the reporter took a statement from a militant, asserting that their motivations were founded in Israel's initial attacks on Palestine. Therefore, the audience hears of Gaza as a victimized region in the context of a conflict in which blame was assigned to both sides. They are acclimatized to the concept of ongoing violence, so Gaza's victimization is less shocking than the vivid introduction of Israeli families hiding from danger.

However, the mention of "a steady stream of wounded arriving [in a hospital in Gaza], including children" (Sawyer & Marquadt, 2012, para. 31) elevates the portrayed victimization of the Palestinians. "Children" belongs to the *VictimCasualties* frame, their innocence inherently evoking sympathy from audiences. Their inclusion in this "steady stream" of victims supports the impression of a people wounded beyond their resources. "Hospital" belongs to the *Recovery* category, as it is a sign of an area that needs support. Such terms are used to suggest a need for sustenance in the face of danger and hurt, which translates to desperation when it is applied to a vulnerable population, such as children.

Furthermore, the juxtaposition of Israel's "iron dome anti-missile system" (Sawyer & Marquadt, 2012, para. 20) with Palestine's "militant rocket-launching site" (Sawyer & Marquadt, 2012, para. 23) highlights a disparity in the coverage of these two sides. The words used in the description of Israel fall into the *Defense* narrative (with the exception of the word "system"), presenting Israel as an entity that is taking action to protect its citizens. Palestine, in contrast, is protected by a "militant" (which belongs to the *Terror* category) "rocket-launching" (which belongs to the *Violence* category) "site," portraying Palestine as an illegitimate, reactive, and violent entity. The word "militant" is commonly used to describe those who commit violence as members of terrorist organizations, thereby delegitimizing fighters who are labelled as such. However, they are portrayed as representative of Palestine, which extends this terrorist designation to the citizens they represent. "Rocket-launching," although categorized under *Violence*, is a manifestation of the *ResponseRevenge* frame because it is presented in the context of Palestinians responding to Israeli attacks with their own violence. This again indicates a people engaged in ongoing conflict, both sides simultaneously portrayed as combatants and as victims. It is a theme used by the media often and effectively in the representation of this conflict, in order to elicit emotional responses from the audience and to provide the sensationalism that supports their interests.

Islamic Terrorism

The presence of Islamic terrorism as covered by American media between 2010 and 2014 consists primarily of periodic threats or potential threats as opposed to acts of violence. The transcript being analyzed (Schieffer et al., 2013) is a prime example of this trend, as it covers a terror threat regarded as serious enough to warrant a travel alert for Americans. The anchor introduces this as the first headline, simply stating, "America on alert" (Schieffer et al., 2013, para. 1). In these first few words, there are two major sentiments at play. The first is designated by the use of "America" as referring to a collective community, an example of the *USWesternWorld* narrative. This narrative presents the Western world and its counterparts as a cohesive state. Stating that America is "on alert" holds further implications for the audience. "Alert" is from the *Defense* narrative, meaning that America must be prepared to defend itself. This unites members of the American community in their need for protection and their fear of violence. Presenting America as a community prepar-

ing to defend itself against an outside force does not merely unite the audience as Americans, however—it unites them against whatever outside force is implementing the threat. These words engage citizens at an individual level and alienate them from whoever is potentially causing the violence, even before that party is introduced in the broadcast. Even the simplicity of this statement, "America on alert," brings a sense of urgency, fear, and panic. It is terse and short, only stating the necessary information. It implies, in this sense, that the threat is so dire that it must be stated clearly and explicitly to inform audiences of the danger.

The first simple statement is followed by the elaboration that, "The State Department warns Americans" (Schieffer et al., 2013, para. 1). "State" is a member of the *LegitimateState* narrative, indicating its role as a source of authority the audience will trust. It is stated that this official department "warns Americans" of the terror threat, indicating a link between the official bureaucracy at the national level and the individual American citizens that are receiving this message. Again, the use of "Americans" identifies listeners as belonging to the community of America, linking the audience to this collective identity. "Warns" belongs to the *Threat* narrative, indicating impending danger. The use of this narrative in addressing the American community relates the danger of the warning to the very nature of this unknown threat, implying an inherent link between the people to whom the threat will be attributed. The use of the *Threat* narrative alienates the audience from the source of the threat and, like the *Defense* narrative, prepares them to protect themselves from the outside force, which is already being framed as an "other."

When the nature of the threat is introduced, it is clearly labeled an "al Qaeda terror threat" (Scheiffer et al., 2013, para. 1). "Al Qaeda," fitting into the United States' view of the *Terror* narrative, is the perpetrator of the threat, made immediately apparent to the audience. "Threat" is a part of the *Threat* narrative, and it functions in the same way as "warns": it evokes a sense of impending danger from an outside force, specified as al Qaeda. *Terror*, as a frame, serves two functions: labeling al Qaeda as a terrorist group and the "threat" as a terror threat. "Terror" in this instance goes beyond the function of clarification; it triggers an extreme response from the audience, based on the recent history of such events (Nacos et al., 2011). The word "terror" in and of itself evokes fear in audiences familiar with events such as 9/11 (Chomsky, 2007). Even those unfamiliar with the events themselves are entrenched in a culture that fears anything categorized as terror, and therefore the word itself is ubiquitous as a catalyst for fear (Chomsky, 2007).

The threat is reintroduced later on in the segment, again as an "alert…for Americans" (Schieffer et al., 2013, para. 13). Repeatedly, this clear statement of a threat addressed directly at the community of America solidifies the dichotomy of a united collective that fears a dangerous outside force. When the correspondent delves into more detail, he reveals that the specific branch of al Qaeda in the Arabian Peninsula (AQAP) is the "most dangerous terrorist organization in the world" (Schieffer et al., 2013, para. 15). Describing this organization as not only dangerous (from the *Warzone* narrative) but as "the most dangerous terrorist organization in the world" is a strong designation. Terms that belong to the *Warzone* narrative assign instability to communities, and when combined with the *Terror* narrative category, suggests a combination of instability, illegitimacy, and ongoing violence. These words describing AQAP relate to the traditional understanding of a terrorist organization as fitting this account, legitimizing hegemonic views of Middle Eastern terrorism and the communities around them. Furthermore, the correspondent states explicitly that an attack from al Qaeda could occur in any "mostly Muslim countr[y]" (Schieffer et al., 2013, para. 15). This identifies the organization with the geographic region of Middle Eastern countries, the religion of Islam, and the people who observe that religion or live in those countries. Such implications are typical of the *IslamMiddleEast* narrative, which expresses that region, religion, and people as a conglomerate "other" relative to the West.

Because of the instability and violence of this conglomerate, the *IslamMiddleEast* narrative expresses the danger of this region expanding or infringing on the West. One manifestation of this is apparent when the correspondent states, "The threat goes beyond U.S. installations to include those of other Western countries" (Schieffer et al., 2013, para. 15). This statement introduces the threat of terrorism against Western embassies in Muslim countries. It

only includes terms from the *USWesternWorld* narrative ("U.S." and "Western"). The correspondent is expanding the defense of safety, threatened by terrorism, beyond American audiences to include citizens of all Western countries. However, there is no mention of the safety of Middle Eastern citizens, no warning that their lives would be threatened by a terrorist attack. This is the result of the *IslamMiddleEast* narrative conglomeration, in which all Middle Easterners are identified as a single given community. AQAP is a defining Islamic organization and the source of the terror threat from the beginning of the report, so its identity as a representation of the Islamic community (and the Middle East) projects the terrorist identity onto the entire Middle Eastern population. Therefore, they are seen as collectively complicit in the terror threat, with no acknowledgment of those Middle Eastern citizens who are at risk of being harmed if the attack occurs.

The correspondent then identified AQAP as a group that "specialized in suicide bombings" (Schieffer et al., 2013, para. 15). Both "suicide" and "bombings" belong to the *Violence* narrative and are terms that are associated with terrorist organizations. Similar terms, such as "bomb," "blew up," and "explosives," occur throughout the remainder of the report, as the correspondent covers past terror attacks and attempts (Schieffer et al., 2013, para. 15). The connection of such specific terms with terrorism and more specifically, AQAP, reminds audiences of these past events that evoke the fear associated with terrorism. Moreover, the correspondent references details of these events and the circumstances thereof, which bring them to mind all the more vividly. All of this pursues the fear of terrorism, a fear that can be brought up by the vague suggestion of an attack and the memory of past violence.

DISCUSSION AND CONCLUSIONS

The results of this study reinforce the conclusions of existing research on media coverage of Islamic acts of violence. The language used in covering these events presents the Middle East as a cultural conglomerate that is defined as the "other" relative to the West. Qualitative analysis illustrates the media's designation of terrorism, instability, and rampant violence as characteristic of Middle Eastern society as a whole. This, of course, is an unrealistic view, but it is veiled within the language that is used to cover terror attacks and, more often, terror threats. Coverage of the Arab–Israeli conflict falls under similar conditions, as shown by qualitative analysis. Typical coverage of this conflict designates this area as a warzone, a setting of ongoing violence that evokes sympathy from audiences. It uses emotional narratives to connect audiences to the victims, while maintaining detachment between the audiences' lives and the struggles of the victims.

However, these are established principles; they are supported by the existing literature that addresses Middle Eastern and Western relations. The macro-analysis stage of this research—the categorization of individual terms into significant narratives—serves to expand textual analysis by melding qualitative bases with quantitative methods. Because it is founded in basic methods (primarily word count), this type of analysis is accessible to all levels of researchers and observers. Furthermore, this methodology is a significant tool that, once established, can be applied to and expanded through future research. It bridges quantitative and qualitative methods, allowing for expansion in a field that has traditionally relied on qualitative, interpretive methods. The establishment of clearly defined narratives relies on accurate categorization of the terms, accomplished through qualitative means. It is at this point that computer programs can be utilized to test the rate and nature of the narratives' occurrences, allowing researchers to analyze larger amounts of data than would be possible without these methods.

These narratives are independent conglomerates that were designed to have standardized contents; that is, they were developed to avoid bias within each given narrative. For instance, the *Palestine* narrative will not include any mention of protest, although research supports a strong presence of such themes in coverage of the Gaza Strip (Wolfsfeld, 2004). These terms instead belong to the *Protest* narrative. Researchers will therefore approach each narrative as a collection of terms related to its heading, according to the definitions provided. Furthermore, the narratives were established specifically to avoid assigning blame at this point in the study. This methodology was developed to take human bias out of the textual analysis and interpretation, in order to maximize reliable and consistent results. The narratives have, at this point, only

been used to calculate word count. This basis will allow for future depth of analysis, such as inferential statistics and association testing.

Testing for correlation and association will allow for clarification into the exact nature of these media frames and their significance. For instance, there has been a recent shift in coverage of the Arab–Israeli conflict from its exclusive portrayal as a struggle between a legitimate state (Israel) and the illegitimate forces that threaten its existence (Palestine) to the introduction of the Palestinians as a people oppressed and victimized by Israel (Chomsky, 2003; Chomsky, 2007; Gilboa, 1987; Wolfsfeld, 1997). Ascertaining the degree of association over time between the frames, *Palestine* and *VictimCasualties,* as opposed to the *Israel* and *VictimCasualties* narratives can determine the exact timing and, possibly, the catalyst of this evolution. In the context of the Middle East, the narratives *LegitimateState* and *IllegitimateState* can be tested against specific countries or political leaders to ascertain which are regarded as legitimate by the American media. An examination of these narratives' relationships will reveal the presence or absence of such trends beyond that allowed by present conjecture. In this capacity, the categorizations are also designed to be transferable to subject matter beyond Islamic acts of violence. They were assembled on the basis of strict definition, so the narratives' presence can be tested on other types of textual analysis, spanning different times, events, geographic areas, and even media. Because these narratives are in the early stages of development, however, their contents will benefit from refinement through future research. This will create more reliable and accurate categorizations, possibly by incorporating existing techniques of text mining utilized in corporate settings.

An expansion on the scope of this research will allow for further examination and comparison of the use of these narratives by expanding the base of texts being examined. For instance, future research can compare the extent to which frames of *Violence* and *Defense* are used in covering acts of Islamic terrorism that occur on American soil as opposed to those that occur in Europe. Furthermore, an expansion of this research will allow for comparisons between networks beyond the national scale to that of local sources. Standardizing narratives in Western coverage allows for comparative analysis against local coverage within the Middle East, which will shed further light on the cultural disconnect and "othering" that occurs. Violence in this region as understood from the local perspective will, if dissected clearly, lead to valuable insights into domestic and foreign understandings of Islamic terrorism, as well as Western intervention and motives. Even outside the scope of Islamic terrorism, further analyses can examine the extent of conflicts between the United States and "hostile" states such as Iran and North Korea, or coverage of past wars with foreign entities. Expanding the timeframe of the study will allow for greater assessment of trends among the narratives, which will in turn expose the shifts in uses of these narratives, rising or falling in response to the times and events. The value of this research lies in its possibilities for future study. The current study has advanced existing techniques of textual analysis, melding it with macro-analysis in order to expand its capacity for accurate and progressive research. These techniques are in the early stages, but they present a new way to assess the presence of media frames, allowing researchers to directly build upon and contribute to textual analysis at a higher level.

REFERENCES

Altheide, D. (1997). The news media, the problem frame, and the production of fear. *The Sociological Quarterly, 38*(4), 647-668. doi:10.111/j.1533-8525.19997.tb00758.x

Bayat, A. (2015). Plebeians of the Arab Spring. Current Anthropology, 56(Suppl. 11), S33-S43. doi:10.1086/681523

Behr, R. L., & Iyengar, S. (1985). Television news, real-world cues, and changes in the public agenda. *The Public Opinion Quarterly, 49*(1), 38-57. doi:10.1086/268900

Bizman, A., & Hoffman, M. (1993). Expectations, emotions, and preferred responses regarding the Arab–Israeli conflict: An attributional analysis. *The Journal of Conflict Resolution, 37*(1), 139-159. doi:10.1177/0022002793037001006

Chomsky, N. (2003). *Middle East illusions: Including peace in the Middle East? Reflections on justice and nationhood.* Lanham, MD: Rowman & Littlefield Publishers.

Chomsky, N. (2007). *Perilous power: The Middle East and U.S. foreign policy: Dialogues on terror, democracy, war, and justice.* Boulder, CO: Paradigm Publishers.

Enders, W., & Sandler, T. (1999). Transnational terrorism in the post-Cold War era. *International Studies Quarterly, 43*(1), 145-167. doi:10.1111/0020-8833.00114

Entman, R. (2004). *Projections of power.* Chicago, IL: The University of Chicago Press.

Gerbner, G. (1977). *Mass media policies in changing cultures.* New York, NY: Wiley.

Gerbner, G. (1988). *Violence and terror in the mass media* (Report No. 102). Paris, France: United Nations Educational, Scientific and Cultural Organization. Retrieved from http://unesdoc.unesco.org/images/0008/000826/082684eo.pdf

Gerbner, G., & Morgan, M. (2002). *Against the mainstream: The selected works of George Gerbner.* New York, NY: P. Lang.

Gerbner, G., Mowlana, H., & Schiller, H. I. (1996). *Invisible crises: What conglomerate control of media means for America and the world.* Boulder, CO: Westview Press.

Gilboa, E. (1987). *American public opinion toward Israel and the Arab–Israeli conflict.* Lexington, MA: Lexington Books.

Gilboa, E. (2002). *The global news networks and U.S. policymaking in defense and foreign affairs* (Report No. 2002-6). Cambridge, MA: The Shorenstein Center on the Press, Politics and Public Policy. Retrieved from http://media.leeds.ac.uk/papers/pmt/exhibits/627/GilboaE.pdf

Gitlin, T. (1980). *The whole world is watching: Mass media in the making & unmaking of the new left.* Berkeley, CA: University of California Press.

Glassner, B. (1999). *The culture of fear: Why Americans are afraid of the wrong things.* New York, NY: Basic Books.

Guskin, E., Jurkowitz, M., & Mitchell, A. (2013). *In the state of the news media: An annual report on American journalism.* Retrieved from http://www.stateofthemedia.org/2013/network-news-a-year-of-change-and-challenge-at-nbc/network-by-the-numbers/

Haklai, O. (2009). Authoritarianism and Islamic movements in the Middle East: Research and theory-building in the twenty-first century. *International Studies Review, 11*(1), 27-45. doi:10.1111/1468-2486.2008-01823.x

Hatemi, P. K., McDermott, R., Eaves, L. J., Kendler, K. S., & Neale, M. C. (2013). Fear as a disposition and an emotional state: A genetic and environmental approach to out-group political preferences. *American Journal of Political Science, 57*(2), 279-293. doi:10.1111/ajps12016

How Americans get their news. (2014, March 17). Retrieved from http://www.americanpressinstitute.org/publications/reports/survey-research/how-americans-get-news/

Hunt, A. (1997). 'Moral panic' and moral language in the media. *The British Journal of Sociology, 48*(4), 629-648. doi:10.2307/591600

Iraq profile – timeline. (2016, December 5). *BBC News.* Retrieved from http://www.bbc.com/news/world-middle-east-14546763

Kruglanski, A. W., & Fishman, S. (2006). Terrorism between 'syndrome' and 'tool.' *Current Directions in Psychological Science, 15*(1), 45-48. doi: 10.1111/j.0963-7214.2006.00404.x

Meadow, R. G. (1973). Cross-media comparison of coverage of the 1972 presidential campaign. *Journalism Quarterly, 50*(3), 482-488. doi:10.1177/107769907305000310

Nacos, B. L. (1994). *Terrorism and the media: From the Iran hostage crisis to the World Trade Center bombing.* New York, NY: Columbia University Press.

Nacos, B. L. (2002). *Mass-mediated terrorism: The central role of the media in terrorism and counterterrorism.* Lanham, MD: Rowman & Littlefield.

Nacos, B. L., & Torres-Reyna, O. (2007). *Fueling our fears: Stereotyping, media coverage, and public opinion of Muslim Americans.* Lanham, MD: Rowman & Littlefield Publishers.

Nacos, B. L., Bloch-Elkon, Y., & Shapiro, R. Y. (2011). *Selling fear: Counterterrorism, the media, and public opinion.* Chicago, IL: University of Chicago Press.

Norris, P., Kern, M., & Just, M. R. (2003). *Framing terrorism: The news media, the government, and the public.* New York, NY: Routledge.

Olmstead, K., Jurkowitz, M., Mitchell, A., & Enda, J. (2013, October 11). *Network: By the numbers.* Retrieved from http://www.stateofthemedia.org/2013/network-news-a-year-of-change-and-challenge-at-nbc/network-by-the-numbers/

Saad, L. (2013, July 8). *TV is Americans' main source of news.* Retrieved from http://www.gallup.com/poll/163412/americans-main-source-news.aspx

Said, E. (1979). *Orientalism.* New York, NY: Vintage Books.

Said, E. (1992). *The question of Palestine.* New York, NY: Vintage Books.

Said, E. (1997). *Covering Islam.* New York, NY: Vintage Books.

Savun, B., & Phillips, B. J. (2009). Democracy, foreign policy, and terrorism. *The Journal of Conflict Resolution, 53*(6), 878-904. doi:10.1177/0022002709342978

Sawyer, D. (Anchor), & Marquardt, A. (Reporter). (2012, November 16). Middle East on the brink: Rain of fire [Transcript of television broadcast]. In *World news with Diane Sawyer.* New York, NY: ABC Network.

24

Schieffer, B. (Anchor), Martin, D. (Reporter), Dahler, D. (Reporter), Mason, A. (Reporter), Quijano, E. (Reporter), LaPook, J. (Reporter), …Hartman, S. (Reporter). (2013, August 2). For August 2, 2013, CBS [Transcript of television broadcast]. In *CBS Evening News*. New York, NY: CBS Network.

Scheufele, D. (1999). Framing as a theory of media effects. *Journal of Communication, 49*(1), 103-122. doi:10.1111/j.1460-2466.1999.tb02784.x

Sheafer, T., & Dvir-Gvirsman, S. (2010). The spoiler effect: Framing attitudes and expectations toward peace. *Journal of Peace Research, 47*(2), 205-215. doi:10.1177/0022343309352110

Suleiman, M. (1974). National stereotypes as weapons in the Arab–Israeli conflict. *Journal of Palestine Studies, 3*(3), 109-121. doi:10.2307/2535896

Timeline: How the Syria conflict has spread. (2014, August 21). *BBC News*. Retrieved from http://www.bbc.com/news/world-middle-east-28850956

Wolfsfeld, G. (1997). *Media and political conflict: News from the Middle East*. New York, NY: Cambridge University Press.

Wolfsfeld, G. (2004). *Media and the path the peace*. New York, NY: Cambridge University Press.

Table 1

Narratives Present in Coverage of Middle Eastern Acts of Violence

Name of narrative (category)	Definition of narrative	Ten most common examples	Total count of occurrences in all transcripts
Terror	Terrorist organizations, individuals, and events	[al] Qaeda, terror, Taliban, ISIS, bin [Laden], terrorist, plot, militants, 911 [9/11], [bin] Laden	22,855
Arab–Israeli	Geographic regions, persons, actions, events, and legislation associated with the Arab–Israeli conflict	Israel, Gaza, Israeli, Hamas, Palestinian, Palestinians, West [Bank], Israelis, Netanyahu, Israel's	22,749
Palestine	Geographic regions, persons, and actions associated with Palestinian territories	Gaza, Hamas, Palestinian, Palestinians, West [Bank], [West] Bank, [Gaza] Strip, tunnels, Palestine, Abbas	11,031
Israel	Geographic regions, persons, actions associated with Israeli territories and Judaic culture	Israel, Israeli, Israelis, Netanyahu, Israel's, [Tel] Aviv, Jerusalem, Jewish, Shalit, synagogue	10,643
VictimCasualties	Identities of victims, conditions of victims	people, man, home, woman, children, school, men, young, kids, women	58,252
Warzone	Military action, destruction/destitution, disputed territories, ongoing conflict	military, war, forces, troops, border, side, soldiers, storm, situation, crisis	34,063
Violence	Violent actions and direct results of those actions	attack, killed, attacks, fire, ground [assault], bomb, hit, death, fighting, fight	57,246
Resolution-Safety	Break in ongoing conflict, emotions, actions associated with that	deal, peace, ceasefire, hope, [peace] talks, safe, [peace] process, pressure, safety, [peace] effort	15,343
Illegitimate-State	Structure and positions associated with illegitimate and undeveloped states and dictatorships	dictator, dictatorship, totalitarian, dictatorships, tyranny, tyrants, despotism, tribesmen, tyrannical, despotic	91
Legitimate-State	Structure and positions associated with legitimate states and democracy	president, rights, country, government, state, officials, national, police, king, secretary [e.g. of state]	63,592
USWestern-World	People, geographic areas, and structure associated with the United States, Western world, and the world at large as referenced by Western media	American, Obama, world, [United] States, United [States], Washington, Americans, America, international, republican	44,339
Defense	Structures, feelings, and actions associated with protection and justified preemptive actions	security, defense, wall, alert, protect, prevent, defend, intercepted, crackdown, defended	7,831

Table 1 cont'd
Narratives Present in Coverage of Middle Eastern Acts of Violence

Name of narrative (category)	Definition of narrative	Ten most common examples	Total count of occurrences in all transcripts
IslamMiddleEast	People, geographic areas, and structure associated with the Middle East and Islamic culture	Afghanistan, [Middle] East, Iraq, Syria, Yemen, Pakistan, oil, Iran, Egypt, Islamic	24,672
Religion	Practices and beliefs associated with religion and religious tenets (precluding those specific to Islam and Judaism)	god, faith, truth, religious, holy, religion, miracle, pray, ideology, prayer	2,221
Response-Revenge	Retaliatory actions in response to initial acts of violence	response, effect, reform, reaction, respond, revenge, backlash, responding, react, retaliate	2,221
BlameIncarceration	Instigators, investigation, incarceration	investigation, evidence, caught, suspect, arrested, investigators, accused, responsibility, charges, cause	16,361
Recovery	Actions and positions associated with recovery aiding victims after violence	help, doctor, hospital, aid, rescue, doctors, build, built, recovery, humanitarian	5,633
Honor	Actions and ideas associated with morality and honor	mission, justice, honor, proud, duty, hero, honest, sacrifice, honored, missions	3,063
FearSorrow-Rage	Reactive emotions associated with the aftermath of acts of violence	fear, memorial, anger, fears, tragedy, afraid, emotional, sad, outrage, scary	4,800
Protest	Actions, ideologies, positions associated with protest	protests, protesters, protest, movement, opposition, activists, activist, resistance, antigovernment, protestors	2,127
Threat	Possible and impending violence	threat, warning, threats, warned, threatening, warnings, threatened, warns, threaten, threatens	4,036

Table 2
Properties of Narratives

Name of Narrative (Category)	Legitimizes entities and their actions	Delegitimizes entities and their actions	Represents area as instable	Describes acts of violence	Provides justification for acts of violence	Reflects perpetrators of violence	Reflects victims of violence
Terror		✓	✓	✓			
VictimCasualties		✓				✓	
Warzone		✓	✓	✓			✓
Violence			✓				
ResolutionSafety						✓	
Illegitimate-State	✓	✓					
Legitimate-State	✓						
Defense	✓				✓		
Response-Revenge			✓	✓			
BlameIncarceration			✓		✓		
Recovery							✓
Honor	✓			✓	✓		
FearSorrowRage					✓	✓	
Protest			✓				
Threat				✓			

An Interview with Dr. Steve Derne, Professor of Sociology

Brendan Mahoney

What's great for you about GREAT Day?

Derne: On GREAT Day students present research that shows an accomplishment in school beyond grades. It shows that they've contributed to sociological knowledge. I'm always impressed by how students rise to the occasion and do professional, focused presentations.

Why does undergraduate research in general matter to you?

Derne: We are teaching students to be sociologists, historians, and physicists. Students understand the process of doing sociology best by actually doing sociology. They learn how to develop interesting questions and ways to answer those questions and they learn how to write papers reporting the results of their research. Completed research projects are the best indication of success in graduate school. Doing undergraduate research helps students gain admission to graduate school.

What's your interest in the specific topic being researched in the following paper?

Derne: Nonordinary, mystic experiences are understudied in sociology and the other social sciences, yet they are an important aspect of the human experience and offer their own wisdoms. Undergraduate research is most helpful in areas lacking much empirical research. These are the areas where students have a real chance to contribute to knowledge.

Near-Death Experience
and the Mystic Path

Felicia Ryan

ABSTRACT

Mukerjee believes that mystical experiences are characterized by feelings of unbounded joy, self-affirmation, self-transcendence, and the mind being free. While these characteristics are not extremely common in our society, certain events may trigger these unfamiliar feelings. Mukerjee's review of paths to mystical experiences did not identify an experience such as near-death. Therefore this study examines four specific characteristics of mystical experiences defined by Mukerjee and looks for these characteristics in documentary evidence of people's accounts of near-death experiences. The study found that near-death experiences, like other mystic experiences, are characterized by unbounded joy, self-affirmation, self-transcendence, and the mind being free.

INTRODUCTION

In our society, nonordinary experiences are not understood with an open mind. Mystical (or nonordinary) experiences are characterized by scholars as having ineffability, passivity, transient and noetic qualities, and a feeling of unity. Mukerjee (1960) believes that sociology can contribute to the weakening of boundaries that suppress unity. The unity in nonordinary experiences can lead to a greater social life and a greater understanding of mystical experiences themselves, thereby enhancing the sociological field.

Throughout the preface of *Theory of Art and Mysticism,* Mukerjee (1960) describes mystical experiences as consisting of characteristics of unbounded joy, self-affirmation, self-transcendence, and the mind being free. Many of these feelings may not be deeply engrained in our cultural society, but can be experienced and seen in everyday life by those who take the time to understand them. People have the ability to partake in mystical types of experiences in their everyday lives, whether it occurs during their yoga class or as a result of a traumatic experience. Triggers of such insight is a subject of debate among scholars. Mukerjee speaks of triggers like starvation, isolation, drug use, hypnosis, elimination of pain, or intense pleasures. Other scholars, like Andrew M. Greeley (1975), include triggers like listening to music, prayer, looking at natural beauty in nature or artwork, quiet reflection, sex, psychedelic drugs, exercise, and many other triggers associated with church. Yet while these triggers have been studied extensively, there are many gaps in the research of mystical experiences. One gap includes looking into the mystical experiences of people who claim to have had visions of the afterlife, which were induced by near-death experiences. The major mystical mindset this study will focus on is one due to having a near-death experience.

Do people who have had a near-death experience claim similar occurrences to that of mystical experiences as described by Mukerjee? Through the study of documentary evidence, this study will analyze the personal accounts of people's near-death experience through analyzing in-depth interviews in the book *Life After Life* by Raymond Moody. This research could potentially lead to a greater understanding and development of both near-death and mystical experiences.

CONNECTION TO LITERATURE

Mukerjee (1960) characterized mystical experience through various qualities he found in his research. He defined mysticism as "the art of inner adjustment by which [a human] apprehends the universe as whole instead of its particular parts" (Mukerjee, 1960, p. xii). What Mukerjee considered products of inner adjustment were the characteristics of unbounded joy, self-affirmation, self-transcendence, and the mind being free. Though he characterized more qualities, I would like to focus my attention on studying near-death experience through the lens of these four characteristics of mystical experience.

The first product of inner adjustment that Mukerjee (1960) characterized was the feeling of unbounded joy. The understanding of oneself as both an individual and as part of a greater whole leads people to feel a sense of joy without boundary. In figuring out oneself, one feels both unity and joy. As Mukerjee stated, "The dialectic of the self moves on from the experience of continuum to that of an undivided Unity or of the world as unbounded Joy" (p. xii). This inner adjustment of a mystical experience recognizes the universe as whole and when seen as whole, it also appears limitless. So, without boundaries, the feeling of joy is endless in mystical experience.

The next two products of inner adjustment Mukerjee (1960) characterized were self-affirmation and self-transcendence. A mystical anxiety about reality supposedly occurs in identifying a person's own consciousness. This accepting of consciousness is what gives an overpowering sense of unity of being through understanding yourself, or as Mukerjee stated, "the participation in the being of others becomes nothing less than the secret of self-affirmation and self-transcendence involved in knowing oneself" (p. xv). In comprehending the universe as a whole, one must affirm their own being. Accepting unity with oneself and the world is where a person must recognize and affirm themselves as valuable individuals in order to participate in this greater whole. Along with self-affirmation, self-transcendence is involved in this process as well. Mukerjee referenced self-transcendence throughout his work, stating that "unlike the [human] of science the mystic's highest effort is an effortless turning inward…by which [s/he] identifies [him/herself] with the wholeness of the universe, transcending time and life," (p. xvi) showing that the highest effort is made without effort. Once one is able to analyze the experience one had, one would have to understand oneself outside the context of time and being in order to fully accept that one had a mystical experience. Then one would be able to understand this deeper unity with the world.

The final product of inner adjustment in a mystical experience is the feeling of a free mind. Mukerjee (1960) notes that "the mind is freed not only from all feelings, including religious or moral sentiments, but also from all notions and concepts," (p. xvii) meaning that people who have had visions of the afterlife become free of previous ties to religious beliefs and have a clean slate of new joy through their mystical experience. Therefore they are open to a new experience that they feel to be both real and effortless.

METHODOLOGY

This study will start by looking at written traces of phenomena, or documentary evidence, of people who have had a near-death experience. I would like to focus on one book by Raymond Moody entitled *Life After Life*, where 100 people were interviewed after they were revived from being clinically dead. Moody's interviews were kept anonymous and therefore no names nor, at times, gender descriptors were presented in introducing information used to describe a near-death experience. The study will focus on whether the experiences were described with a more emotionally descriptive vocabulary, concentrating on the four characteristics that Mukerjee described as unbounded joy, self-affirmation, self-transcendence, and the mind being free. For unbounded joy, the study will see if the person highlights a limitless sense of happiness, joy, bliss, delight, ecstasy, etc. For self-affirmation, this study will see if the person asserted strongly that what they felt was right, true, genuine, or factual. For self-transcendence, the study will look to see if the person's near-death experience was beyond a normal and physical realm of being. Then the study will look to find if the person said phrases similar to, "It was nothing like I have ever experienced before," or "It was out of this world." Lastly, for looking at the mind being free, this study will seek out feelings of clarity from the person or belief that their judgment was free from internal questioning. I will use these four preliminaries as a base to be able to fully interpret the person's descriptions of their near-death experience. After collecting data, this exploration aims to contribute to a better understanding of near-death experiences and how they fit into Mukerjee's mysticism.

FINDINGS

Near-death experience provided feelings of unbounded joy. The first person described their own experience in which they saw deceased family members like so: "It seems that I mainly saw their faces and felt their presence. They all seemed pleased. It was a very happy occasion, and I felt that they had come to protect or to guide me" (Moody, 1975/2001, p. 50). The next person focused even more on the euphoria of their experience: "I enjoyed going through this flashback. That was fun. I had a good time going back to my childhood, almost like I was reliving it. It was a way of going back and seeing it which you ordinarily just can't do" (Moody, 1975/2001, p. 62). As another person described, "I approached [the mist] more closely, I felt certain that I was going through that mist. It was such a wonderful, joyous feeling; there are just no words in the human language to describe it" (Moody, 1975/2001, p. 72). The "mist" this person was talking about was the line he described between visions of him and his deceased family members. He found joy in his near-death experience when he began to be with his family members who had already passed away. The last person, in the throes of their experience, believed that "the doctor had already said that I was gone, but I lived through it. Yet the experience I had been through was so joyous, I had no bad feelings at all" (Moody, 1975/2001, p. 74). This person had a more general feeling of joy based on his whole mystical experience. Each of these quotes is an account of joy using descriptions like wonderful, enjoyment, happy, joyous, etc. What they have in common with one another is that this type of happiness was used to describe their visions of past experiences. Whether it was in visions of their youth or visions of their loved ones through a near-death experience, they each felt a sense of joy. They understood themselves and their visions allowed them to be happy in context of being whole with their past experiences. The sense of joy did not seem to be described explicitly without boundary, like Mukerjee (1960) characterized, but the joy in understanding oneself through a near-death experience is seen in these people's near-death experiences.

Near-death experiences also had a sense of self-affirmation. The first person claimed that "while I was out of my body, I was really amazed at what was happening to me. I couldn't understand it. But it was real" (Moody, 1975/2001, p. 77). When speaking about their near-death experience they described themselves as being out of their physical body, and while they could not make full sense of it they understood it as a real experience. The next person described their experience as:

> Nothing like an hallucination. I have had hallucinations once, when I was given codeine in the hospital. But that had happened long before the accident which really killed me. And this experience was nothing like the hallucinations, nothing like them at all. (Moody, 1975/2001, p. 78)

This person was defending their experience as something real—not as something people would normally dismiss as a hallucination. They even compared it back to when they truly did hallucinate, and understood their near-death experience as more than that. Lastly, as another person claimed:

> I didn't tell anyone about it for a long, long time. I just didn't say anything at all about it. I felt funny about it because I was afraid that nobody would think I was telling the truth, that they would say, "Oh, you're making up these things." (Moody, 1975/2001, p. 79)

This person was nervous to tell others about their near-death experience because they were afraid of what those others might think. They did not want someone to say that they were making things up, because in their mind they were telling a true account of something that was real to them. Each of these accounts is self-affirming in that the participants strongly asserted that what they felt was right, true, genuine, or factual. They were not describing their experience as something like a dream but as an actual experience. They recognized their own experiential value and did not want other people to tell them what they faced or did not face—they knew that their near-death experience was genuine. While there was no interpretation of comprehending the universe as a whole like in Mukerjee's (1960) understanding of self-affirmation, each of these people did support their own being by affirming themselves as a valuable individual who understood their near-death experience as true.

Near-death experiences also had qualities of self-transcendence. The first person stated, "I had a floating sensation as I felt myself get out of my body, and—I looked back and could see myself on the bed below and there was no fear" (Moody, 1975/2001, p. 34). This person had an experience they described as out of the physical realm of being, where they felt and could see themselves out of their body. The next person claimed that

> I kind of lost my sense of time, and I lost my physical reality as far as my body is concerned—I lost touch with my body. My being or my self or my spirit, or whatever you would like to label it—I could sort of feel it rise out of me, out through my head. (Moody, 1975/2001, p. 43)

This person lost their sense of all reality and that of the physical and normal realm of being. As another person described, "my being had no physical characteristics, but I have to describe it with physical terms. I could describe it in so many ways, in so many words, but none of them would be exactly right. It's so hard to describe" (Moody, 1975/2001, p. 44). This person had a difficult time describing what they felt in their near-death experience, but they were beyond any physical being. The last person stated that "I have been somewhere nobody else has ever been" (Moody, 1975/2001, p. 81). This person believed that they went somewhere that no one had ever experienced before and were therefore out of reality. All of these accounts showed that these people transcended their own lives and understood themselves out of the context of physical being. Unlike Mukerjee's (1960) idea of self-transcendence, none of these people claimed a deeper unity with the world, although their conception of overcoming the limits of their individual being were clearly outlined.

Near-death experiences showed characteristics of the mind being free. One person described their near-death experience simply like this: "I just had a nice, great feeling of solitude and peace…It was beautiful, and I was at such peace in my mind" (Moody, 1975/2001, p. 26). This type of peace of mind showed some sort of freedom of mental thought. Another person described this peace of mind as a "darkness was so deep and impenetrable that I could see absolutely nothing but this was the most wonderful, worry free

experience you can imagine" (Moody, 1975/2001, p. 30). This appears to show that while the person's mind was stimulated by darkness, they were worry-free, which showed a sense of freedom in their mind. Lastly, as a person described, "things that are not possible now, are then. Your mind is so clear. It's so nice" (Moody, 1975/2001, p. 46). This person described their mind being clear during their near-death experience as compared to when they were back in reality. All of these accounts showed feelings of clarity and freedom from terrestrial concepts. While this clarity was engrained in Mukerjee's conception of the mind being free, it did not as described include any feelings of freedom from religious or moral feelings as well. The people did have this sense of a free mind that was at peace with itself and their being.

CONCLUSION

The purpose of this research was to address the question of near-death experiences having similar characteristics of mystical experiences as described by Mukerjee (1960). The study focused on the characteristics Mukerjee described as unbounded joy, self-affirmation, self-transcendence, and the mind being free. What was found through this research of documentary evidence was that near-death experiences did consist of the qualities of unbounded joy, self-affirmation, self-transcendence, and the mind being free. The conclusion drawn from this collection of data showed that near-death experiences can be categorized as mystical experiences. Though further research would need to be done to further prove and elaborate on these findings, the content of this research shows that near-death experience and mystical experience tend to have similar characteristics.

REFERENCES

Greeley, A. M. (1975). *Sociology of the paranormal: A reconnaissance*. Beverly Hills, CA: SAGE Publications.

Moody, R. (2001). *Life after life*. San Francisco, CA: Harper Collins. (Original work published 1975)

Mukerjee, R. (1960). *The theory and art of mysticism* (2nd ed.). Bombay, India: Asia House.

An Interview with Taylor Powers, Student Author

Brendan Mahoney

What's great for you about GREAT Day?

Powers: Most of the academic college experience revolves around learning new information and acquiring skills pertaining to one's field of choice. But at some point, it becomes essential that the students apply what they have learned in a more practical sense. Unfortunately, in many colleges and universities across the United States, this opportunity is not provided until the graduate level. But that is what is so unique about SUNY Geneseo and GREAT Day. Students are able to delve into a research project of their own choosing, fostering an environment of independent discovery amongst their own peers.

What impact do you think GREAT Day has on our campus culture?

Powers: Not only does GREAT Day foster an environment of active, practical learning, but it also creates a campus culture in which the opinions and interests of the students are highly valued by their professors and their peers alike. It is not a new idea that an atmosphere conducive to learning must engage the students at a level beyond the standard classroom lecture, but GREAT Day takes the concept further, demonstrating that the College is genuinely interested in the students and what they have to offer to their prospective fields. Consequently, when the faculty and staff prioritize the research, talent, and professional development of their students, the entire campus in turn puts a high value on active involvement—both in the academic world and in the surrounding community.

Why does undergraduate research in general matter to you?

Powers: Personally, I think that independent research or directed study is an invaluable component of the undergraduate experience. Not only does it allow students to think more critically about what they have learned, but it also teaches them that they can be actively involved in their field from the beginning of their studies. Curiosity and discovery do not require a master's degree or PhD, and as such, it is disadvantageous to confine a student's education to a traditional classroom setting until the graduate level—especially because many students do not pursue a degree beyond their bachelor's.

What's your interest in the specific topic being researched in the following paper?

Powers: From a young age, I have always had a strong interest in foreign languages, but during my under-graduate career, I ended up discovering that I was also interested in the actual process of second language acquisition. With society becoming more and more globalized, it is becoming more advantageous for people to be bilingual. However, in order to be able to teach a second language, one must first understand the lin-guistic framework of acquisition, how the mind processes language, and how it is subsequently produced. Just as with one's first language, the acquisition of a second language is strongly influenced by the learner's environment. As such, I wanted to discover what effect the learning environment has on the acquisition of pronunciation. If we are more aware of what influences a student's acquisition, then we will in turn be able to teach more effectively, more efficiently, and in a more personalized manner.

Non-Native Speaker Perception of Native Speaker Dialect Authenticity and Implications for Pedagogy

Taylor Powers

ABSTRACT

Extensive research has been conducted on second language acquisition and its perceived limits. Many will argue that these limitations, such as age of acquisition, can be counterbalanced by certain factors of motivation. If an individual has an internal desire for native-like use of the language, then hypothetically they should be better equipped to reach such a level. But how do these motivational factors develop, and what factors from the learning environment could be responsible for fostering them? This study was designed to explore the influence of non-native speaker perception of native speaker dialect authenticity and its implications for pedagogy. If an individual perceives a dialect to be more authentic than another, could this influence their desire to obtain a manner of pronunciation similar to the favored dialect, as directed by their perceived future L2 self? It was hypothesized that the dialects that differ more from neutral Spanish—in other words, those that exhibit more distinct phonemes—would be deemed more authentic and would be used as a personal basis for measuring and directing acquisition. Statistical analysis showed significant correlations between dialectal preference and those who have Spanish-speaking family and friends, as well as those who intend to study abroad. These results suggest that students who are not exposed to specific dialects prior to formal education may not be fully aware of dialectal variance and as such they may not be able to make an educated decision in their own pronunciation acquisition.

INTRODUCTION

For many years, the Critical Period Hypothesis (CPH) has been used to describe the potential for authentic pronunciation in second language acquisition. The theory states that there is a particular age prior to pubescence at which the ability to attain phonetic authenticity is optimized (Johnson & Newport, 1989). After the onset of puberty, it is further hypothesized that the ability to obtain this authenticity drops off dramatically as the individual progresses into adulthood. As further studies have been conducted and have disproved the CPH (Flege & Yeni-Komshian, 1999), it has been determined that many other factors are involved in acquisition, the majority of which extend far beyond the proposed limitations of age and the associated decrease in mental plasticity. An example of a factor that has been studied as a counterbalance to acquisition limitations is motivation. According to the future L2-self model proposed by Dörnyei and Chan (2013), each L2 learner has a self-created image in their mind of how they perceive themselves using the language in the future. This "future self" image helps to guide their acquisition, acting as a visual motivation for the attainment of their linguistic goals (Dörnyei & Chan, 2013).

The study was designed to look at the exposure that second-language students have to Spanish dialectal variance and how this experience may work in conjunction with their future L2 self as a means of directing their pronunciation acquisition. In other words, do students have a certain dialect that they prefer, and if so, do variables such as age of acquisition, length of study, exposure to native-speakers of particular dialects, or factors of motivation affect this preference?

It was hypothesized that the dialects which differed the most from neutral Spanish (or those that exhibited more distinct phonemes) would be ranked higher than more conservative dialects, and that these dialects would ultimately be used as a guide for individual pronunciation acquisition as directed by the future L2-self model.

METHODOLOGY

Participant Demographics

For this study, a diverse group of participants was established from the Spanish Language and Literature Department at the State University of New York at Geneseo, a public liberal arts college. Of the 197 participants, a wide demographic range was represented.

Table 1. Participants Demographics, Course Numbers, and Age of Spanish Acquisition.

Gender	
Female	59%
Male	41%
Age	
18	18%
19	27%
20	22%
21	23%
22	6%
23+	4%
Course Number	
Low-Level (100, 200)	59%
Upper Level (300+)	41%
Spanish Age of Aquisition	
≤12	17%
>12	83%

Procedures

Students in 10 Spanish courses of seven levels were offered the opportunity to participate in the study. These courses ranged from introductory Spanish to literature and linguistics lectures (Table 2). For the purposes of this study, they were divided into lower-level and upper-level categories. Participation involved the completion of a questionnaire that asked for basic demographic information and inquired about individual exposure to the Spanish languages and native speakers as well as motivation for learning the language. Additionally, participants were asked to listen to 10 recordings[1] of 10 different speakers reading a short story in Spanish. For each, they ranked

1 Recordings were borrowed with the permission of Dr. Carlos-Eduardo Piñeros and the University of Iowa from the "Dialectoteca de Español" database.

the authenticity of the speaker's pronunciation on a scale of 1 to 5, with 1 representing a recording that they deemed to be least like a native speaker, and 5 representing a recording that they perceived to be most like a native speaker. Eight of the speakers were native Spanish speakers, each exhibiting a different dialect, and two were non-native controls.

Table 2. Participating Spanish Course Numbers

Course #	Title	Level
101	Elementary Spanish I	Lower
102	Elementary Spanish II	Lower
201	Intermediate Spanish I	Lower
300	Oral Communication	Upper
302	Hispanic Literature	Upper
306	Latin American Literature	Upper
323	Linguistics	Upper

Recordings

The eight native speaker recordings included the following dialects: Mexico (Mexico City), Costa Rica (San José), Colombia (Bogotá), Peru (Trujillo), Chile (Punta Arenas), Spain (Barcelona), Venezuela (Caracas), and Uruguay (Minas). Because it is difficult and often controversial to define a standard version of a language, it seemed more practical to distinguish the native speaker recording from one another based on neutrality. A neutral dialect is one that tends to be phonologically conservative, meaning that it adheres more to orthography by minimizing the number of phonological processes.

Table 3. Non-Neutral Recordings. The native speaker recordings that were said to be non-neutral due to a higher number of phonological processes and unique phonemes.

Dialect	Process	Phone
Mexican	Aspiration of /s/	[h]
	zheismo	[ʒ]
Costa Rican	dzheismo	[dʒ]
Chilean	aspiration of /s/	[h]
	palatization of /x/	[ç]
Uruguayan	aspiration of /s/	[h]
	sheismo	[ʃ]
Peninsular	velarization of /x/	[χ]
	distinction	/θ/
	apical s	[s̺]
Venezuelan	aspiration of /s/	[h]
	velarization of final /n/	[ŋ]
	elleismo	/λ/

This can be compared to a radical dialect that exhibits many phonological processes, making the spoken language more different from the written language. Based on this distinction, the dialects of Colombia and Peru were said to be the most neutral while the other six were said to possess enough unique phonemes and phonological processes to make them diverge from neutrality (Table 3).

Method of Analysis

The information obtained through the questionnaires and recording rankings was coded and analyzed using SPSS. The non-numerical questionnaire data was analyzed primarily by correlations (chi-squared McNemar for nominal-nominal correlations and chi-squared eta for nominal-interval correlations). The recording rankings were averaged and compared using a one-way ANOVA/Tukey HSD analysis.

RESULTS

Recording Analysis

The mean ranking of each recording was calculated and plotted to show the relationship between the native dialects and the non-native controls (Table 4).

Rank	Reecording #	Mean	Dialect
			Table 4: Recording Means and Overall Rankings
1	10	4.5436	Venezuela
2	7	4.4745	Uruguay
3	4	4.2857	Colombia
4	5	4.2704	Peru
5	1	4.1385	Mexico
6	6	4.0969	Chile
7	8	3.7755	Spain
8	2	3.4592	Costa Rica
9	9	1.7857	Non-Native (F)
10	3	1.1429	Non-Native (M)

A one-way ANOVA/Tukey HSD analysis was then used to test whether a significant difference existed between each recording. It was found that the non-native controls and the Costa Rican and European Spanish dialects had significantly lower ($p < 0.01$) average rankings when compared to those with higher averages (Figure 1).

To determine if course number was significant, the upper-level Spanish students were analyzed separately for their mean ratings of the 10 recordings. When compared to the rankings of all of the participants, there was a slight shift in the order of the means (Table 5). Venezuelan, Uruguayan, and Colombian remained the three dialects with the highest perceived authenticity. However, the Chilean recording was

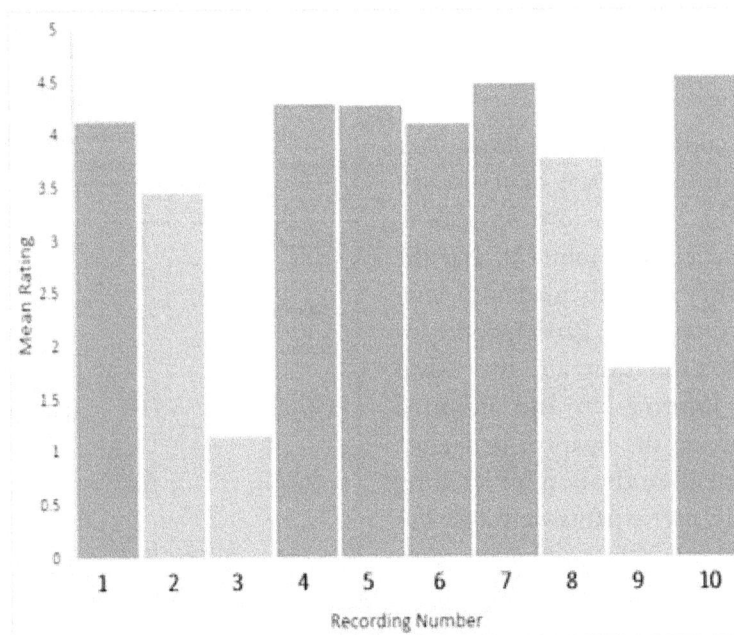

Figure 1. Recording Mean Rankings. Recordings that were found to have significantly lower averages than those above them (2, 3, 8, and 9) are marked in green ($p < 0.01$).

ranked higher in the upper-level courses, resulting in a drop in rank for the Peruvian and Mexican dialects. The bottom two dialects remained the same (Peninsular Spanish and Costa Rican), with the non-native controls falling below them.

Table 5: Rankings of Upper-Level Recording Means			
Rank	Reecording #	Mean	Dialect
1	10	4.7848	Venezuela
2	7	4.5625	Uruguay
3	4	4.4875	Colombia
4	6	4.375	Chile
5	5	4.3375	Peru
6	1	4.2125	Mexico
7	8	3.8	Spain
8	2	3.6625	Costa Rica
9	9	1.5125	Non-Native (F)
10	3	1.025	Non-Native (M)

A one-way ANOVA/Tukey HSD test was used to find any significant differences between the values, and it was determined that only the two non-native speaker controls were significantly lower ($p < 0.01$) than the other recordings (Figure 2). As such, no significant difference was observed between the eight Spanish dialects.

It is also interesting to note that the non-native speaker controls were significantly different from one another ($p < 0.01$) when looking at all participants together *and* when analyzing the upper-level students separately.

Dialectal Preferences

As a part of the questionnaire, participants were asked to check a box next to the dialect that they would want to sound like. Options were also given to write in another dialect that had not been suggested or to indicate no preference. Of those who had a preference, a noteworthy percentage selected Mexican and European Spanish (Figure 3).

Because approximately 40% of the participants showed a specific dialectal preference, the factors that could potentially affect a second language learner's dialectal choice were analyzed. Using a series of chi-squared correlations, the non-numerical questionnaire data was compared to the presence of absence of a preference. It was found that an individual is more likely to not have a preference if they are taking Spanish as a program requirement ($p = 0.023$), if Spanish is not their major ($p = 0.000$), if they do not intend to study abroad ($p = 0.032$) or live abroad ($p = 0.036$), and if they do not have Spanish-speaking friends ($p = 0.002$) or family ($p = 0.000$). It is also interesting to note that no correlations were observed between having a dialectal preference and age of acquisition, length of study, past study abroad or live abroad experience, and the desire to obtain native-like pronunciation, despite that these factors were hypothesized to be significant.

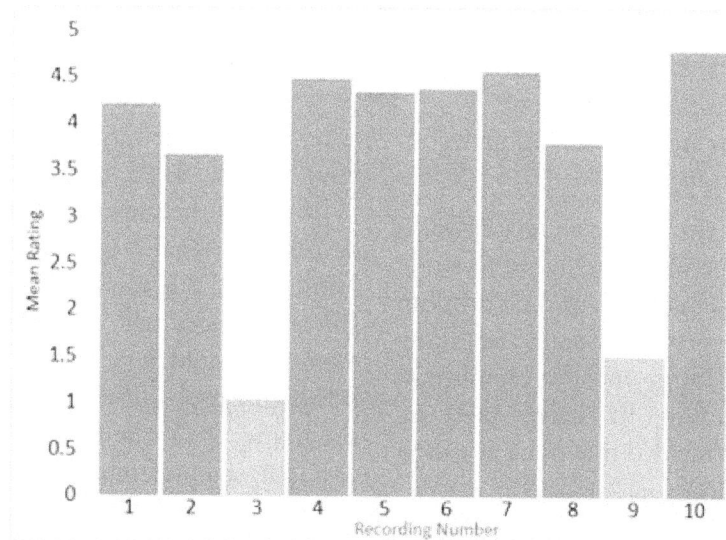

Figure 2. Upper Level Recording Means. Recordings that were found to have significantly lower averages than those above them (3 and 9) are marked in green (p < 0.01).

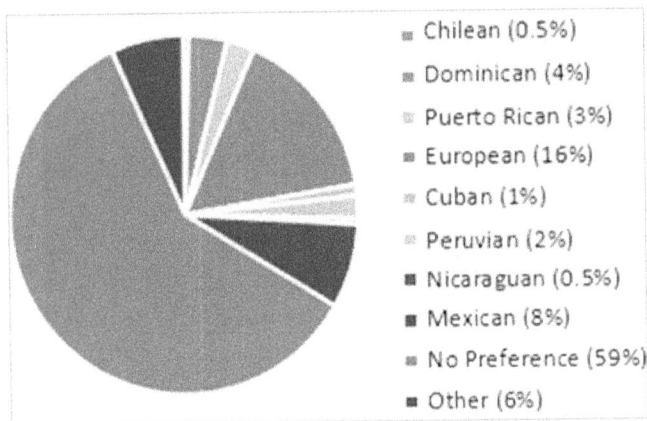

Figure 3. Dialectal Preferences. While more than half of the participants had no preference, those that did showed an inclination toward Mexican and European Spanish.

After looking at factors affecting the presence or absence of a preference, the decision was made to look further into what factors may influence the selection of specific dialects. Using chi-squared analyses, the following correlations were observed:

- If a student wants to have native-like pronunciation, they are less likely to prefer Chilean ($p = 0.025$).

- If a student isn't learning Spanish because of Spanish-speaking family, they are less likely to prefer Dominican ($p = 0.000$) or Puerto-Rican ($p = 0.000$).

- If Spanish is not the student's major, they are less likely to prefer Peruvian ($p = 0.012$) or Mexican ($p = 0.021$).

- If a student isn't learning Spanish to study abroad, they are less likely to prefer European Spanish ($p = 0.008$).

From these correlations, two apparent relationships were observed, the first between the desire to study abroad and the preferential selection of the European dialect, and the second between Spanish-speaking family as a motivational factor and the Dominican and Puerto-Rican preferences. To analyze these results further, the data was divided into two groups on the basis of age of acquisition: <12 and ≥12.

Separate correlations revealed two new relationships:

- If a student has a desire to study abroad, they are more likely to have an age of acquisition greater than or equal to 12 ($p = 0.018$).

- If a student has a higher age of acquisition, they are less likely to have Spanish-speaking family ($p = 0.004$).

As such, there seems to be a relationship between a lower age of acquisition, the presence of Spanish-speaking family members, and a preference for Dominican and Puerto-Rican Spanish. Similarly, a relationship is possible between a higher age of acquisition, a desire to study abroad, and a preference for European Spanish.

CONCLUSIONS

Recording Rankings

When we look at the results for the overall recording rankings, we can see a significant difference between European and Costa Rican Spanish when compared to the other dialects. However, when the upper-level students were analyzed separately, we saw a rise in the ranking of these two dialects until they were no longer significantly lower. From this, we can conclude that students with more exposure to the language are able to distinguish between native and non-native speakers but don't have a tendency to differentiate between native speakers.

Dialectal Preferences

While we observed several correlations between various motivational factors and dialectal preferences, one of the most interesting was the probable relationship between age of acquisition, specific dialectal preference, and expected use of the language in the future. First, we saw that a lower age of acquisition seemed to be tied to the presence of Spanish-speaking family as a motivational factor and the preferences of Dominican and Puerto-Rican Spanish. It is understandable that those who have Spanish-speaking family members would have a lower age of acquisition, since it is highly probable that the language was spoken in the home. It can be further suggested that the specific dialectal preferences are the result of the country of origin of those family members. For the higher age of acquisition group, we saw the desire to study abroad as a motivational factor and the preference of European Spanish. Many of the students within this group began learning Spanish at the age of 12 or shortly after. In a large portion of grade schools within the United States, it is common to begin learning a second language at this age. It is also highly probable that these individuals only began learning the language later in life because they did not have exposure to it at a young age, that is, because they do not have Spanish-speaking family. Therefore, we can see that many of these students are hoping to gain more in-depth exposure to the language through study abroad. That being said, it is interesting to see a preference for the European Spanish dialect. We can hypothesize that this is the result of a desire to study abroad in Spain, although this would need to be confirmed through further analysis.

Another correlation we observed was between students with a Spanish major and the Peruvian and Mexican dialectal preferences. It is interesting to note that the college from which these students were selected offers study abroad programs to Peru and Mexico that are available for upper-level students. From this, we can hypothesize that students who have a desire to study abroad in a specific country may wish to have a dialect similar to the one spoken in the target country.

Additionally, the correlations discussed above can be connected to Dörnyei's Future L2-Self Model. We are seeing that students who hope to use Spanish in the future, either as a means of communication with their family members or as a resource when studying abroad, are showing specific dialectal preferences that relate to the target country and associated dialect. Therefore, it seems that expected use of the language may provide a guide for acquisition.

Implications for Pedagogy

From what we have observed, it seems that students may benefit from increased exposure to dialectal variance at an earlier age. If students are aware of the variation in pronunciation that exists within their target language, they may be able to make a more informed decision when directing their linguistic acquisition. What we often see is a dichotomy between Latin America and Europe in which second language students see all Spanish-speaking countries within Central and South America as very similar, when in fact they offer a diverse wealth of cultural and phonological variance. Similarly, we see that students are unaware of how ubiquitous the Spanish language is, often forgetting that Africa has a Spanish-speaking country and that the United States itself has a wide variety of dialects represented. It appears that if we educate students from a younger age on the variability of language, and if we provide a more accurate depiction of the cultures themselves, then students will be better prepared for their future use of the language.

REFERENCES

Johnson, J. S., & Newport, E. L. (1989). Critical period effects in second language learning: The influence of maturational state on the acquisition of English as a second language. *Cognitive Psychology, 21*(1), 60-99. doi:10.1016/0010-0285(89)90003-0

Flege, J. E., Yeni-Komshian, G. H., & Liu, S. (1999). Age constraints on second-language acquisition. *Journal of Memory and Language, 41*(1), 78-104. doi:10.1006/jmla.1999.2638

Dörnyei, Z., & Chan, L. (2013). Motivation and vision: An analysis of future L2 self images, sensory styles, and imagery capacity across two target languages. *Language Learning, 63*(3), 467-462. doi:10.1111/lang.12005

An Interview with Kaitlyn Morgan, Student Author

Brendan Mahoney

What's great for you about GREAT Day?

Morgan: What makes GREAT Day so special is that it gives students an opportunity to showcase their hard work at Geneseo. It's a wonderful way to share ideas with our fellow students and expand our knowledge. We get to not only better our own speaking and research skills, but also learn from our peers about topics we may never have researched ourselves.

What impact do you think GREAT Day has on our campus culture?

Morgan: GREAT Day creates a campus culture of knowledge sharing and continuous learning. It's just as important to learn from our peers as it is to learn in a classroom. It encourages students to take a break from being wrapped up in their own curricula and appreciate what other students around them are doing. It's easy to forget that so much more is happening on campus when you're focused on your own work, and GREAT Day allows students to expand their horizons past that.

Why does undergraduate research in general matter to you?

Morgan: Undergraduate research has given me the skills necessary to be a Peace Corps Volunteer. It has taught me to think critically and analyze a topic from all different aspects. The skills I gained during my research on doulas has carried over into Rwanda, as much of what I do requires me to monitor and evaluate my community in order to make life-saving changes. Without my directed research, I would've never been able to try to address the issues in my community now.

What's your interest in the specific topic being researched in the following paper?

Morgan: I have been interested in "alternative" (non-medical) birth practices since my Freshman year at Geneseo. Childbirth is a wonderfully beautiful process that is fascinating to me. I became curious why medical interventions seemed so necessary to a completely natural process. It was then that I decided I wanted to be a midwife, and I switched my focus from a biological standpoint to an anthropological one. Many midwifery journals suggested the use of a doula in childbirth to reduce stress, and I knew I had to learn more, leading to me eventually becoming a doula in the process of doing this research.

Not Just for "That Kind of Mom": An Ethnographic Analysis of the Perceived Benefits of Childbirth Doulas in Rochester, New York

Kaitlyn Morgan

ABSTRACT

Since the origin of childbirth, a female attendant has accompanied a woman in labor. As time progressed, these attendants began to receive special training, and became professionally known as doulas. The twentieth century has brought an increasing demand for highly medicalized birth practices, with hospital births and caesarian sections at an all-time high. The ability of a woman's body to naturally have a baby has been overshadowed by these practices, forcing many women to feel it is necessary to seek these methods in order to have a safe birth. This ultimately creates a realm of fear surrounding childbirth in America. Alternative birth practices, such as those where doulas are present, may be able to become more common if increased knowledge of doulas is available. Studying doulas allows for the identification of factors that contribute to a woman's choice to use a doula.

INTRODUCTION

Since the origin of childbirth practices in America, a female attendant has accompanied a woman in labor (Papagni & Buckner, 2006). As time progressed, these attendants began to receive special training, and became professionally known as doulas. The word doula is derived from the Greek word meaning "a woman who serves" (DONA International, n.d.). Originally, they assisted the mother after birth with breastfeeding (Papagni & Buckner, 2006). Today, these women have expanded their practices to offer many supportive roles to both mothers-to-be and hospital staff.

The twentieth century has brought an increasing demand for highly medicalized birth practices, with hospital births and caesarian sections at an all-time high (Menacker & Hamilton, 2010). The ability of a woman's body to naturally have a baby has been overshadowed by these practices, forcing many women to feel it is necessary to seek these methods in order to have a safe birth. This ultimately creates a realm of fear surrounding childbirth in America. Studying doulas allows for a better understanding of the support that doulas offer and their benefits to the women who use them, enabling the practice to become more common.

OBJECTIVES AND RESEARCH QUESTIONS

The first objective of this study is to gain a better understanding of the roles of childbirth doulas, specifically in Rochester, New York. This study also aims to analyze personal testimonies from women who have chosen to have doula-attended births regarding why they felt that this was the best option for them. The perspective of doulas themselves is taken into consideration as well in order to further understand their roles. Lastly, this study focuses on the perceived benefits of childbirth doulas in helping both women and hospital staff achieve a mother's desired birth goals.

This research attempts to answer four main questions:

- What are the perceived benefits of doula-attended births for mothers, and why do women opt to have a doula present during childbirth?

- What factors influence women's decisions to use doulas?

- What do doulas themselves think influence women's decisions to use a doula, and what do they do to address those issues? and

- How do hospitals accept and accommodate the roles of doulas, and are they well-accepted?

FIELD SITE

The research was conducted in Rochester, New York. Rochester is located in Western New York and has a population of roughly 210,000 people (U.S. Census Bureau, 2013). The estimated median household income of Rochester inhabitants is $30,158, which lags behind the state average median income of $57,369 (City Data, 2013). Throughout Rochester, there are pockets where many people live below the poverty line. The people living in these low-income areas are more vulnerable to lack of access to health care, including, but not limited to, birth attendants such as doulas.

There are currently 40 to 50 doulas in the Rochester area. However, only 20 to 25 of these doulas are actively taking referrals and practicing. Out of these 20 to 25, 10 to 15 doulas are not consistently taking clients. This leaves roughly a dozen doulas who have consistent clientele of more than one client a month.

My main focus was on the Beautiful Birth Choices (BBC) birth center located within the city. BBC offers doula support and training, as well as prenatal yoga, childbirth classes, and several other prenatal and postnatal services (BBC Rochester, 2015). This birth center is close to several hospitals in Rochester and has close ties to the midwifery group. I also attended the Doula Organization of North America (DONA) doula training course at BBC in June 2015, as participant observation.

METHODS AND RESEARCH PARTICIPANTS

This research used qualitative and ethnographic methods in order to investigate the perceived ben-

efits of childbirth doulas. I began my research with an extensive review of the literature available on doulas. Upon review of the literature, I focused my research on my four main questions. I then attended the DONA doula training course at BBC and took in-depth notes on the process of becoming a doula, as well as witnessed firsthand the support offered by a doula. The training took three days to complete, each day consisting of roughly eight hours of hands-on training.

Following my participant observation, I created semi-structured interview guides in order to introduce conversation topics while ultimately allowing the interviewees to direct the flow of conversation. I interviewed a sample of women falling into four categories: women who have used a doula (n=2), mothers-to-be who have not previously used a doula but are going to for their birth (n=2), hospital staff who have worked with doulas (n=2), and doulas themselves (n=2). Additionally, I interviewed my key informant, one of the coordinators at BBC. Women were chosen based on referrals from my key informant. After the first round of interviewing, several interviewees gave me suggestions on whom to interview next. I also consulted the Doula Cooperative website to find doulas in the Rochester area. The names of the interviewees have remained anonymous and confidential throughout the entire research process. For this reason, pseudonyms have been given to each participant referenced in this paper.

All of my interviewees were white females living in the Rochester area. Out of the nine participants, six had been trained as doulas (my key informant, the doulas themselves, both hospital staff members, and one mother). Ages of participants ranged from 27 to 58, with most participants in their early to mid-30s. This sample generally had a high level of education. Eight out of nine participants had at least a bachelor's degree, three participants had master's degrees and one had a Juris Doctor. Only one participant did not complete college. All women were middle to upper-middle class.

CHALLENGES AND SUCCESSES

This research posed a few challenges. The biggest challenge was finding research participants who were willing to be interviewed. Several of the potential interviewees did not respond to emails or phone calls. It was also difficult to schedule interviews around busy work schedules. A minor challenge was travelling to Rochester several times a week.

There were many successes throughout this project. I was able to hear incredible stories from these women about their unique birth experiences. My interviewees were each very helpful and knowledgeable when discussing birth, which allowed the conversation to flow easily and organically. I also found great success in listening rather than fully directing the interviews. I was able to put aside my own biases about doulas and let the interviewees express their opinions without judgment. Initially I thought this would have been the biggest challenge but I found I was able to listen better than I had thought.

Main Arguments

The research resulted in three main discoveries. First, the data suggests that childbirth doulas are beneficial to mothers before, during, and after labor. I argue that doulas offer several benefits that other health care providers do not. The ultimate result of this support is the alleviation of fear, as I will discuss in this paper.

The second argument is that doulas are well-accepted in hospitals. I argue that there is an overwhelmingly positive hospital perception of doulas. Doulas and hospital staff occupy complimentary, rather than opposing, roles.

Finally, in this paper I will argue that there are two key factors that affect a woman's choice to use a childbirth doula. The first is misconception of what a doula does and the types of births she attends. The second deterrent is economic. The cost of a doula's services and the inability of a woman to afford a doula may be a large part of why women aren't using the doulas that are available to them in the area.

Literature Review

According to DONA International, a doula has seven main roles:

- to "recognize birth as a key life experience";
- to "understand the physiology of birth and the emotional needs of a woman in labor";

- to "assist the woman and her partner in preparing for and carrying out their birth plan";
- to "stay by the side of the laboring woman throughout the entire labor";
- to "provide emotional support, physical comfort measures, an objective viewpoint, and assistance to the woman in getting the information she needs to make good decisions";
- to "facilitate communication between the laboring woman, her partner, and clinical care providers"; and finally
- to "perceive the doula's role as one who nurtures and protects the woman's memory of her birth experience" (DONA International, 2015).

Amy Gilliland (2006) argues that doulas have five main roles. Many of these overlap with those suggested by DONA International. Additional roles include covering neglected areas in care left by busy hospital staff and facilitating a team atmosphere that welcomes collaboration between the doula, hospital staff, mother, and partner.

As Simkin and Way argue, one of the doula's main objectives should be to offer "informational support" (as cited in Chapple, Gilliland, Li, Shier, & Wright, 2013, p. 58) in which she relays information to the mother in terms that she can understand more easily. This is extremely important in times of stressful labor when the woman may not be thinking clearly. The doula must be able to translate what the doctor is saying so that the woman can focus on the birth itself.

Additionally, the doula helps the birth go more smoothly by supporting the partner as well. Amy Gilliland (2014) states that this takes the pressure off of the partner and allows them to experience the birth in a different way than if they were worrying excessively about supporting their wife. However, it is important that the doula does not displace the partner's role, but rather compliments it with additional support. The partner also generally has a lot of anxiety during labor and can benefit from the presence of a doula (American Academy of Pediatrics [AAP], 2004).

Several studies focus on the statistical analysis of the benefits of birth doulas to women. One such study by Papagni and Buckner (2006) concluded that "childbirth interventions are currently at an all-time high" (p. 12). Additionally, as of 2002, the Caesarian birth rate was at 24%, the induction rate is 44%, epidural use is 63%, and the episiotomy rate is 52% (Papagni & Buckner, 2006). Infections and other complications are common following a Caesarian birth, as it requires a major open surgery (Davis-Floyd, 2005). Gilliland (2014) stated that doulas help to reduce the Caesarian birth rate by 50%. They also reduce the epidural rate by 47% and the episiotomy rate by 24%. The overall labor time is shortened as well (Gilliland, 2014).

Qualitatively, doulas help to reduce the negative perception of birth that some women may have (Bruggemann, Parpinelli, Osis, Cecatti, & Neto, 2007). DONA International (2015) argues that women who have a doula present during labor have reduced negative feelings toward their childbirth experience. Having a doula present also decreases anxiety of both the mother and the father, and may contribute to a lower number of women with postpartum depression (Papagni & Buckner 2006). In a study done by Bruggemann et al. (2007), women who had used a doula rated their labor and delivery with higher satisfaction than those who did not have one present.

Another benefit for women using a birth doula is that the doula can offer one-on-one care and attention to a mother when a nurse is not available. Due to the increase in the medicalization of birth, nurses have other tasks to attend to rather than offering undivided emotional and psychological support to the mother. The nurse must be able to attend to multiple patients at once, leaving little time to tend to the mother's individual needs (Papagni & Buckner, 2006). In fact, labor and delivery nurses usually allot only 10% of their time to support of the mother beyond medical care during labor. Doulas are able to focus on one woman at a time and can put aside complicated medical issues in order to focus directly on the woman's needs (AAP, 2004).

Lastly, studies have shown that there is an economic benefit to using a birth doula. A study done in Wisconsin in 2010 reported that in-hospital doula support saved an average of $424.14 per birth (as cited in Chapple et al., 2013). Also, insurance companies are more willing to cover doula costs now because they save money if women can avoid C-sections, epidurals, and longer hospitalization due to complications or long labors (Preparing for Birth, n.d.).

Doulas have generally been well received by hospital staff and their popularity continues to grow. According to Lantz, Low, Varkey, and Watson (2005), 69.6% of doulas feel they are respected by physicians and nurses working in labor and delivery. This, however, still leaves a significant amount of doulas feeling unwelcome in the delivery room.

One of the biggest concerns of nurses regarding doulas is that their presence may take away the role of the nurse as a supporter. Another concern is that the doula will actually make the nurse's job more difficult by creating obstacles or conflicts in opinion (Gilliland, 2014). Often, the animosity toward doulas is a result of confusion regarding the roles of doulas by the hospital staff. This uncertainty in roles creates issues for both parties (AAP, 2004). The nurse's negative attitude toward the doula may cause a negative birth experience for the mother if gone unaddressed (Papagni & Buckner, 2006).

The doula's role is meant to be complimentary to both the family and medical staff (AAP, 2004). Case studies have reported that when the relationship between the hospital staff and the doula are cohesive, the birth experience is more positive when rated by mothers (Papagni & Buckner, 2006). When creating a positive birth environment, Gilliland (2014) believes that it is important to include all parties to support the woman in labor. The doula/nurse relationship is meant to be a collaboration, not a tug-of-war.

Unfortunately, there is a tremendous amount of "not knowing" (Davis-Floyd, 2005, p.38) surrounding birth in the United States. Davis-Floyd (2005) argues that birth activists fight to give women more options during birth other than the common highly medicalized practices of American doctors. Women may not know that alternatives are available to them, such as doula support. There is a misconception that "doctors 'know' that they are giving women 'the best care'" (Davis-Floyd, 2005, p. 38), but while they are knowledgable, every woman is different and entitled to options to make the best choice for themselves.

Perceived Benefits of Doulas

Doulas offer several benefits to women that enable them to achieve their goals during birth. Perhaps the largest benefit to women who use a doula is continuous support. The support offered by hospital staff is often interrupted by busy schedules and medical procedures. According to an AAP Case Study (2004), hospital staff in labor and delivery may only be able to offer 10% of their time to each individual mother during her labor. In contrast, DONA International (2015) states that one of the main roles of a doula is to "stay by the side of the laboring woman throughout the entire labor."

My research supports that doulas remain with their mother the entire time she is laboring. Eight out of nine participants in this study discussed continuous support as the key benefit a doula could offer a mother. "Joanna," a twenty-seven-year-old mother of a newborn baby girl, expressed her gratitude toward her doula's continuous support, stating, "She was literally on me every single contraction. She was on my hips, in my face...just to feel so much better about it all" (personal communication, October 2015). Joanna went on to tell me that during her long labor her doula never left her side, a commitment that lasted nearly 17 hours:

> I think she ended up coming over around midnight that night.... The midwife was called at three in the morning and she got there at five. And then my birth lasted until three [that afternoon] and she [the doula] was hanging out until five. So she was there the entire time. (personal communication, October 2015)

This continuous support manifests in three forms, or layers, repeated throughout the personal testimonies I collected. These layers provided by doulas are informational, physical, and emotional support. Several participants expressed that it was this kind of all-encompassing continuous support that alleviated fear and anxiety. I will discuss the benefits of each of these and how they alleviate fear in the following sections.

Informational Support

DONA International (2015) states that informational support should be one of the top priorities of a doula. This informational support can be provided before, during, and after labor. Before labor, mothers seek information on what to expect in addition to confirmation that everything is normal when their bodies are changing. Furthermore, a doula is able to work almost as a translator between hospital staff and mother. Often, hospital staff members use jargon that women do not understand. A doula is able to clarify complicated medical terms for her client (Chapple et al., 2013). Doulas are knowledgeable on birth and medical procedures, and can answer any questions their mothers might have.

Doulas in this study confirmed that one of their main goals was to offer informational support to mothers. One doula, "Martha," discussed her vast collection of resources that she could distribute to mothers if they had any questions prior to labor. Martha also said that often her clients had questions in the weeks following birth, and she made herself readily available to answer these questions (personal communication, September 2015). Another doula, "Rosie," who had been practicing since 2006, stated that her informational support came mainly in the form of "bringing knowledge of birth other than medical knowledge" (personal communication, November 2015). Rosie found that a doula often has experience with aspects of labor itself that doctors don't always see because the doctors aren't in the room for the entire process. She is able to provide relief from anxiety and fear by answering questions throughout labor, even after the doctor or nurses have left. She is also able to clarify medical procedures for her clients.

Additionally, there were a large number of mothers in this study who believed informational support was a key component of their doula care. One mother-to-be, a thirty-three-year-old lawyer named "Anna," remembered her doula telling her from the beginning that "if you don't know what your options are, you don't have any" (personal communication, September 2015). Anna relied on her doula for alternatives to medical births so that she could choose the best option for her. Her doula then continued to send her resources that helped her overcome her fears of attempting a vaginal birth after Caesarean (VBAC).

"Rachel," a mother of two who had chosen a doula for her second birth, described her doula as "setting the tone" for her birth by providing her with information that reduced her fear after her stressful first birth experience:

> She [her doula] set the tone in advance. We talked about all my fears from the first birth and she gave me resources to learn about creating a peaceful environment…. She recommended books. She used tools to show me how to spin the baby in my pelvis. It was a good reminder of how birth works. (personal communication, September 2015)

Physical Support

The literature suggests that physical support by a doula greatly benefits a woman in labor. A doula can help a mother walk around or get into a warm tub. She can also offer calming massages or counterpressure in order to make the mother more comfortable (Green, Amis, & Hotelling, 2007). Doulas also offer breastfeeding support immediately after birth in order to help facilitate latching (BBC Rochester, 2015).

Perhaps the largest positive of physical doula support is that it often leads to fewer medical interventions. Doulas help to decrease the Caesarian rate by 50%, a huge benefit when Caesarians are more expensive than vaginal births. In addition, a doula's physical support can reduce the epidural rate by 47%, leading to healthier babies through natural childbirth practices (Gilliland, 2014).

Two mothers in this study, Rachel and Joanna, both greatly attributed their successes in intervention-free births to their doula's physical support. Rachel stated that her doula "encouraged me to do things I wouldn't have naturally done on my own," such as walking up the stairs sideways in order to open her pelvis (personal communication, September 2015). Since Rachel's baby was turned sideways originally, this technique helped Rachel avoid a Caesarian due to a breech position of the baby. Rachel's doula also encouraged her to breathe with open lips, which helped her to concentrate on breathing rather than the pain.

Joanna discussed her doula's physical support in helping to turn her baby as well. She said her doula was very knowledgeable on how to reposition the baby and prevent breech position. Joanna's doula was also by her side during each contraction to offer counterpressure. At the end of the interview, Joanna told me that without her doula, she would have definitely wanted to go to the hospital and have an epidural because her labor was so intense and long.

Instead, Joanna was able to avoid any medical interventions and had a beautiful home birth.

> I feel I couldn't have done it without her…. She [her doula] was like 'Honey, I know, I know what you're going through.' I felt she knew that the pain was normal. She was literally on me every single contraction. She provided me with the techniques to get through it. (personal communication, October 2015)

Physical support leads to the alleviation of fear surrounding Caesarian births. Both Joanna and Rachel knew they did not want a Caesarian birth but were afraid that hospitals would push them to have one. Joanna even opted to have a home birth because she was so nervous about a Caesarian. Rachel and Joanna were able to feel more comfortable throughout labor due to their doula's physical support, which reassured them that they would not need medical intervention.

Emotional Support

The last layer of support offered by doulas is emotional support. This support can help reduce the negative perception of birth that women may have (Bruggemann et al., 2007). DONA International (2015) states that a doula's role is to help reduce negative feelings toward childbirth, assuring the mother that her experience was a positive one. Emotional support also manifests as soothing words, which assure the mother that labor is normal. This can reduce fear and anxiety, especially when a woman has negative perceptions about labor going into it (Papagni & Buckner, 2006). Emotional support can also lead to a higher feeling of satisfaction after birth (Bruggemann et al., 2007) in addition to lower rates of postpartum depression (Papagni & Buckner, 2006).

Doulas offer emotional support mainly through the constant reassurance that everything is normal and okay. "Emily," a midwife, believes that moms are able to rely on their doulas for emotional strength during difficult labor:

> Moms look to their doulas. Like when the going gets really tough…it is so common for me to see a mom look to her doula and just get the strength she needs. These little moments, looks, comments, all make a profound difference and impact in a woman's birth experience. I think that's what being a doula is all about. I see these moments a lot. That's the real power and value. (personal communication, November 2015)

One mother, Rachel, described her doula's presence as "empowering" and reassuring (personal communication, September 2015). She knew that she was going to be alright due to her doula's constant emotional support. Martha, a doula, put it best: "The biggest thing is reassuring the mom that everything is okay. Usually everything is okay, and if it's not, it will be" (personal communication, September 2015). It's this kind of emotional support that enables women to get through labor with less fear and anxiety.

Emotional support is also prominent after birth. Doulas will usually meet with their clients roughly one-to-two weeks after the birth to go over the birth experience with the mom and help her work through challenging parts she may not have come to terms with. Often, moms frame their birth in their minds as somewhat of a failure. Martha said that during her postpartum visit, women often express that they perceive their birth experiences negatively and are hard on themselves about how they handled labor. She said it is her job to help them work through this and reframe the birth in a positive way (personal communication, September 2015). In fact, Joanna said that she was very negative until her doula visited her after the baby was born. Joanna said that her doula just looked at her and said, "Are you kidding? You were amazing! Your labor was hard and you got through it how you needed" (personal communication, October 2015). This made all the difference to Joanna, who had a very long and exhausting labor.

OTHER BENEFITS
Partner Support

A case study by the AAP (2004) suggests that the woman's partner also has a great deal of anxiety while the mother is in labor. The partner is readying themselves to become a parent as well. They also may not be able to handle seeing their partner in pain and may not know how to help. A doula can clarify the role of the partner and offer suggestions for support.

Furthermore, a doula's support takes pressure off of the partner. This allows them to have their own birth experience. The partner does not need to worry about the mother being unsupported if a doula is present as well (Gilliland, 2014).

My key informant described her own birth as "more balanced" when a doula was present in addition to her husband (personal communication, June & October 2015). She said that her husband, doula, and midwives created a support team that felt whole. The doula helped her husband integrate into the birth team and collaborated with him on how to support her (personal communication, June & October 2015).

Hospital staff members and mothers who had used a doula already felt that doulas gave partners much-needed breaks during labor. Labor can be exhausting for all parties involved. One mother recalled her husband being more in need of her doula at times than she was. Her husband was exhausting himself and the doula helped to calm him down and made sure he was eating or sleeping throughout the long labor. Both mothers who had used a doula also said that their husband didn't need to feel like he had to protect her because the doula did that.

> My husband is introverted and a guy, so of course he wants to be the only one to provide for me. He didn't think he'd be able to be himself with a doula in the room. But he was able to be more supportive because he knew I was being taken care of by another person, too. He was able to emotionally support me. He had gotten so exhausted during our first. (Rachel, personal communication, September 2015)

Because of this support for the partner, women interviewed felt their husbands were able to be emotional supporters to them and remain calm. One doula, Rosie, even joked that she's had partners say that every dad needs a doula just as much as the woman in labor (personal communication, November 2015).

HOSPITAL STAFF PERCEPTION

Both the literature and my research point to an overwhelmingly positive perception of doulas among hospital staff members. Doulas and hospital staff members collaborate on how to best help a mother through labor, with a doula's role complimenting that of a nurse (AAP, 2004). This creates an overall more positive birth experience for the mother (Papagni & Buckner, 2006).

However, some negative perceptions still surround doulas in the hospital setting. Negative perceptions of doulas usually come from misconceptions of a doula's roles by hospital staff (AAP, 2004). Hospital staff may be unsure as to what a doula is there for or may think that the doula is overstepping her role. Furthermore, a doula may be perceived as a threat to a nurse's role. A nurse may feel that a doula is creating more problems than solutions because she is in the nurse's way (Gilliland, 2014).

In this study, two hospital staff members were interviewed: a midwife named Emily and a labor and delivery nurse named "Saige." Both Emily and Saige felt that doulas contributed positively to the birth team. Emily said that she had "99% of the time— totally positive experiences" when working with a doula (personal communication, November 2015). Overall, Emily believed doulas collaborated with hospital staff rather than undermined them:

> It makes my job a lot easier as a midwife when my patient has a doula. I don't have to worry about them getting through labor. A doula can help the mom through each contraction or give her partner a break. I feel more comfortable with one there. Moms need a great support team. (personal communication, November 2015)

Saige expressed to me the mutual respect she found between doulas and nurses. She said that she was comfortable that a doula would be helpful, respectful, and supportive. It was nice for her to know that she could trust a doula to continue to support her patients even when she couldn't be in the room. Additionally, doulas respect a nurse's position and aim to complement their differing, yet equally important, roles (personal communication, November 2015).

Neither doulas nor hospital staff members interviewed mentioned negative personal experiences working with each other. Emily did say that she had heard from doctors or nurses that patients tend to be more demanding with a doula present (personal communication, November 2015). Sometimes hospital staff may not want to deal with a demanding patient and they blame the doula for this. Saige agreed that doulas are perceived as "obstructive" when their patients argue with hospital staff over their birth plan (personal communication, November 2015). Doulas are often falsely blamed for making their clients too demanding. Despite this misconception, doulas were still generally perceived as having a positive impact according to hospital staff members.

DETERRENTS

Misconceptions

Davis-Floyd (2005) argues that women often are under the impression that hospital births attended by doctors are the best option for mothers. They also hold many misconceptions about birth because they do not know their options or are fearful of alternatives. This is due to the over-medicalization of birth in the United States. For birth activists, choice is the most important thing for women during their birth experience, and options give them that autonomy. Activists aim to help women not miss out on their ideal birth just because they didn't know their options for support (Davis-Floyd, 2005).

Interestingly, many of the women interviewed during this study mentioned this lack of awareness and general misconceptions as major deterrents from choosing doula support. The main misconception stems from the idea that doulas are for "that kind of mom." "Gloria," a 35-year-old mother-to-be, told me that there was a lot of misinformation out there that women are reading, and this creates unnecessary fears that push women to choose hospital births. She said that these women often think doulas will make them have a home birth or a natural birth, and this scares them into not choosing a doula (personal communication, September 2015). Another mother-to-be, Anna, almost didn't choose a doula because she was under the impression they were for home births and she wanted a hospital birth for her higher-risk VBAC. Anna didn't even know doulas were an option for someone in her situation:

> That's how it was the first time around. I just accepted whatever option was presented to me because I didn't know of any alternatives. What I like about doulas is that they can take more time with you than doctors can to help you make these decisions. (personal communication, September 2015)

Rachel and Joanna, who have already used doulas, also said that many women they have spoken to think a doula will make them have a natural birth. Joanna said she was often looked at as a "crunchy granola" mom, a mom who practices alternative and natural medicine, when she talked about using a doula (personal communication, October 2015). In actuality, doulas are for every kind of mom. My key informant said that a doula's job is to support moms in whatever they desire (personal communication, June & October 2015). A doula does not push natural birth practices on women; she facilitates a positive birth experience for her client in whatever way she can. Whether it's a home birth or a hospital birth, a doula's purpose is to continuously support the mother in her decisions. This is best exemplified in my key informant's vision for Beautiful Birth Choices:

> Our motto is "inform, empower, support." It's not just about natural births. It's about getting information into people's hands so they know their choices. We want to be able to support mothers in any context that they want. We want to tell them all of their choices and then we want to support them in whatever that looks like. We just want to help moms reach their goals, always with healthy moms, healthy babies in mind. The support picture is where everything else

comes from. (personal communication, June & October 2015)

Another misconception is that a doula and a midwife do the same job for a mother. Many women ask, "If I have a midwife, why do I need a doula?" In short, a midwife is a health professional who takes care of the medical aspects of a birth. She may also offer other forms of support, such as emotional or informational, but those are not the primary goals of her care. She may also have several patients she is dealing with at once in the hospital or birth center, so her care may be divided among them. In contrast, a doula focuses on their client's emotional and mental health throughout the entire labor. She provides continuous support in ways a midwife may not be able to. A doula also does not do anything medical.

Economic Barriers

Much of the literature reviewed seemed to find doulas affordable and economically beneficial. According to a Wisconsin study, doula support can save roughly $424 per hospital birth. This is due to a decrease in medical interventions and shorter hospital stays (Chapple et al., 2013). In addition, according to Preparing for Birth (n.d.), insurance companies are willing to cover doula care in many cases. This is due to the amount of money doulas save insurance companies by avoiding Caesarean births and epidurals, which can be rather costly.

However, in contrast with the literature, cost and ability to afford a doula may be the largest deterrent in choosing a doula for the women of Rochester. The women I interviewed who had chosen to use a doula were all able to afford one as they were all educated and married (providing another source of income). In reality, Rochester is known for its low-income areas and pockets of poverty. For those women, affording a doula may be close to impossible.

According to my key informant, "there's nothing set in place to provide a lot of low-cost or gratis doulas to moms" in Rochester (personal communication, June & October 2015). Currently, most insurance companies do not cover doula care for the women of Rochester. There are some resources available to pay for doulas but these are not well known. Often, new doulas will do gratis work in order to get their certifications, and women can hire them for free. Again, many women do not know this is an option. Some women may qualify for The Birth Partners program that allows them to have an in community doula free of cost, but even this is only available for a certain period of time. Ultimately, without the help of insurance companies, low-income mothers are not able to afford doulas and opt to not have one.

CONCLUSION

In Summary...

As suggested by both the literature and this study, childbirth doulas are highly beneficial to women throughout their entire birth experience. The support offered by doulas can come in many forms, and is tailored to each woman's specific needs. The three most common forms of support are informational, physical, and emotional. Each of these layers of support contributes to reducing the fear and anxiety surrounding overly medicalized births that many women are faced with.

In addition to supporting a mother, a doula also supports her partner. This further contributes to a more relaxing birth environment for both the mother and partner. By incorporating the partner into the doula's role, a more balanced approach is reached.

As births are becoming more medicalized, it is important that hospital staff and doulas are working together in collaboration. Hospital staff perception has been overwhelming positive in the Rochester area. Doulas and hospital staff work together on the same team in order to create an optimal birth experience for their mothers with limited stress.

Unfortunately, there are some deterrents from choosing to use a childbirth doula. Many women are unaware that a doula is an option. They may also not know exactly what a doula does or may think they don't need one if they have a midwife. Additionally, there are a lot of misconceptions surrounding doula support, including that doulas are for home births or women who don't believe in medical interventions. In actuality, for doulas it is important that women are not limited in their options and are able to have the birth they desire. Doulas support all kinds of moms and all kinds of births. Doula's are not just for "that kind of mom," but rather, for every different kind of mom.

For the women of Rochester, economic constraints limit many women from access to a doula. When money is an issue, women may not choose to make doula support a priority for where to distribute their funds. Insurance companies also may not cover doula care, making it unaffordable to low-income women.

Points of Further Research

After studying the Rochester birth community, it would be interesting to learn more about programs available to low-income women to afford doula care. My key informant mentioned that there are some programs available but these are not well known to many women. Studying these programs could help to understand why women do not have access to them and gain a better insight into how many are available.

It would also be beneficial to study partner perception of doulas. Several women expressed their surprise at how much their doula helped their partner get through the birth. I would like to interview partners and ask how they perceive doula support.

Lastly, further research on insurance companies may prove useful, especially for the women of Rochester. For example, I want to know why insurance companies aren't choosing to cover doula care and if there are any companies that are working toward doing so. Since Caesarian births are more expensive and the rate is high, it would behoove insurance companies to cover doula care as an alternative.

Broader Implications

This study could be used to bring about more awareness of doulas in the Rochester area. It may encourage doulas to advertise more and clear up many of the misconceptions surrounding their services. With more awareness, more women may choose to use a doula.

Additionally, this study could aid in grant writing to train more doulas in Rochester. Through these grants, gratis doulas could be offered to low-income mothers. It would also enable doulas in community to be trained to work with mothers in community, something that is lacking currently for low-income areas with a diverse group of women.

A Doula for Every Mom

There is a saying from the doula training I attended that has stuck with me: "there is a doula for every mom." The doulas of Beautiful Birth Choices are working hard to provide doula support to women from every walk of life with every kind of birth plan. It is important that women feel supported throughout birth, a natural process that has been made to seem scary due to its medicalization. Doulas can alleviate this fear and empower women to do exactly what their bodies were made to do. I imagine that there will come a time when there will be a doula for every mom—not just higher-income moms or "crunchy granola" moms, but every mom who needs one. But first we must work to dispel the misconceptions surrounding doula support, and make them affordable and available to women.

References

American Academy of Pediatrics. (2004). Benefits of a doula present at the birth of a child. *Pediatrics, 114*(5), 1488-1491. doi: 10.1542/peds.2004-1721R

Beautiful Birth Choices Rochester. (2015). *Beautiful Birth Choices*. Retrieved December 29th, 2015, from http://www.bbcroc.com/bbc/

Bruggemann, O. M., Parpinelli, M. A., Osis, M., Cecatti, J. G., & Neto, A. (2007). Support to woman by a companion of her choice during childbirth: A randomized controlled trial. *Reproductive Health, 4*(5), 1-7. doi:10.1186/1742-4755-4-5

Chapple, W., Gilliland, A., Li, D., Shier, E., & Wright, E. (2013). An economic model of the benefits of professional doula labor support in Wisconsin births. *Wisconsin Medical Society, 112*(2), 58-64. Retrieved from https://www.wisconsinmedicalsociety.org/_WMS/publications/wmj/pdf/112/2/58.pdf

City Data. (2013). *Rochester, New York*. Accessed December 29th, 2015. Retrieved December 29th, 2015, from http://www.city-data.com/city/Rochester-New-York.html

Davis-Floyd, R. (2005). Anthropology and birth activism: What do we know? *Anthropology News, 45*(5), 37-38. doi:10.1525/an.2005.46.5.37

DONA International. (n.d.). *For mothers and families*. Retrieved May 18th, 2015, from http://www.dona.org/mothers/index.php

Gilliland, A. (2006). Beyond holding hands: The modern role of the professional doula. *Journal of Obstetric, Gynecologic, and Neonatal Nursing, 31*(6), 762-769. doi:10.1177/088421702129005416

Gilliland, A. (2014). Commentary: Nurses, doulas, and childbirth educators—working together for common goals. *Journal of Perinatal Education, 7*(3), 18-24. Retrieved from www.amygilliland.com/pdf/commentarygoals.pdf

Green, J., Amis, D., & Hotelling, B. A. (2007). Care practice #3: Continuous labor support. *Journal of Perinatal Education, 16*(3), 25-28. doi:10.1624/105812407X217110

Lantz, P. M., Low, L. K., Varkey, S., & Watson R. L. (2005). Doulas as childbirth paraprofessionals: Results from a national survey. *Women's Health Issues, 15*(3), 109-116. doi:10.1016/j.whi.2005.01.002

Menacker, F., & Hamilton, B. E. (2010). *NCHS data brief: Recent trends in cesarean delivery in the United States*. Retrieved from https://www.cdc.gov/nchs/data/databriefs/db35.pdf

Papagni, K., & Buckner, E. (2006). Doula support and attitudes of intrapartum nurses: A qualitative study from the patient's perspective. *The Journal of Perinatal Education, 15*(1),11-18. doi:10.1624/105812406X92949

Preparing for Birth. (n.d.). *Doulas can improve the health of both mother and newborn*. Retrieved from www.prepforbirth.com/user/BT%20how%20doulas%20help%20handout.doc

U. S. Census Bureau. (2013). *Rochester, NY Demographic Information*. Retrieved December 29th, 2015, from http://quickfacts.census.gov/qfd/states/36/3663000lk.html

An Interview with Dr. Tze-Ki Hon, Professor of History

Brendan Mahoney

What's great for you about GREAT Day?

Hon: GREAT Day is great because it turns the whole college into a gigantic conference center and gives students and staff the opportunity to learn, to explore, and to discover new knowledge. In one day, everyone is a learner, regardless of their rank, role, and responsibility.

What impact do you think GREAT Day has on our campus culture?

Hon: The effect of GREAT Day on campus culture is enormous. It reminds everyone (students, faculty, and staff) of what SUNY Geneseo stands for. It is not just a place to work or to get a bachelor's degree. Rather, it is a place of learning where the liberal arts environment nurtures and develops the beautiful mind.

Why does undergraduate research in general matter to you?

Hon: To me, the purpose of undergraduate research is not the research result. Frankly, the four-year college does not provide enough training and knowledge to students to make ground-breaking discoveries. Those new discoveries are made in the PhD programs. Instead, the purpose of undergraduate research is to give students a sense of what it looks like to be a researcher, encouraging them to continue learning after graduating from college. In this sense, GREAT Day is extremely important in showing what comes next after graduation.

What's your interest in the specific topics being researched in the following two papers?

Hon: In "'New China, Great Olympics': A Historical Study of the 2008 Beijing Olympic Games" I was impressed by Thomas Garrity's acute sensitivity to collective memory. In the paper, he focuses on an enduring memory among the Chinese—China is the "Sick Man of Asia" due to a century of continuous defeats by foreigners. This memory has been passed from generation to generation in schools, novels, cinemas, television programs, and more recently, animated games. What Garrity shows in his paper is the massive expression of this national anxiety in international sports competitions. Sometimes this national anxiety could push athletes to work harder to achieve a better result, but in other times this national anxiety could be a tool of the Chinese government to garner domestic support (e.g., the 2008 Beijing Olympics). Whether it is for personal glory or national pride, Garrity argues that international sports in China are arena for national redemption where "the Century of Humiliation" ends and "the rise of China" begins.

In "*Fist of Fury* or *Drunken Master*: Masculinity, National Identity, and Modern China," I was intrigued by Peter Benson's creative use of the martial arts movies to elucidate the drastic changes in the Chinese national identity from Mao's China to post-Mao China. Methodologically, Benson is unique in the sense that he connects three separate fields of study—the study of movies, the study of Chinese nationalism, and the study of masculinity. More significantly, he connects the three fields under the context of China's great transformation from a socialist planned economy to an innovative market economy serving neo-liberal global capitalism.

"New China, Great Olympics": A Historical Study of the 2008 Beijing Olympic Games as a Spectacle that Promoted Chinese National Strength on an International Stage

Thomas F. Garrity

Abstract

The Chinese treated the 2008 Beijing Olympic Games as a spectacle that reestablished China's strength on the international stage. In order to relieve the historical shame of the Century of Humiliation from Chinese historical memory, the Chinese felt the need to both win and host international sporting events. To showcase a "New China," the Chinese modernized Beijing's transportation infrastructure, attempted to reform the manners of its citizens, and sought to dominate the medal count of the sporting events in order to broadcast the image of a newly strengthened, modern nation to the international community. The political motivations of the CCP led the 2008 Beijing Olympic Games to be utilized as a spectacle to promote the image of "New China, Great Olympics," and showcase Chinese national strength on an international stage.

The Chinese treated the 2008 Beijing Olympic Games as much more than a mere international sporting event. The official Chinese Communist Party (CCP) commentary set the stage for the highly anticipated 2008 Beijing Olympic Games, stating: "Beijing will stun the world with the most successful sporting event it has ever seen, striving to compose the most dazzling chapter yet in Olympic history" (as cited in Lovell, 2008, p. 767). This prideful declaration sought to grandly debut China as an Olympic host. The Beijing Games were to be the spectacle that reestablished China's strength on the global stage. For what reasons would the Chinese seek to utilize this international platform for such a nationalistic purpose?

The use of the Beijing Games in this manner was grounded in two underlying causes: the shame embedded in recent Chinese history, and the CCP's political motivations. The modern Chinese people are burdened by the shameful historical memory of the Century of Humiliation in which their nation was militarily defeated by Western imperial powers in the Opium Wars of the 1840s and by Japan in the Sino–Japanese War of 1894-1895. This is what caused China's struggle for self-identification, as the Chinese began to perceive their nation as merely one among many in a "Social Darwinist" struggle for survival. This led the Chinese to establish a strong connection between the strength of their nation's populace and the strength of the nation on the international stage. Thus, the 2008 Beijing Olympics were to be the spectacle that proved to the global community that China was no longer the "Sick Man of East Asia."

The desire to prove Chinese strength on the international stage also aligned with the political motivations of the CCP. Once Deng Xiaoping rose to preeminent leadership of the CCP in the late 1970s, he drastically shifted the party's focus away from communist doctrines to more pragmatist policies. Thus, the authoritarian party's legitimacy to rule could no longer rely upon Maoist ideology and was instead tied to a variety of factors, most importantly, popular nationalism. One means by which to generate this popular nationalism was through success in international sport. Thus, the CCP sought to utilize the Beijing Olympic Games as a spectacle to showcase China's national strength in order to satisfy its political goal of generating popular nationalism for its own legitimacy. The desire to use the Games to promote national strength is best demonstrated by the official slogan of "New China, Great Olympics," which was indicative of China's desire to showcase its recently regained national strength and its ability to successfully host a grand international event. To showcase a "New China," the Chinese modernized Beijing's transportation infrastructure, attempted to reform the manners of its citizens, and sought to dominate the medal count of the sporting events in order to broadcast the image of a newly strengthened, modern nation. Furthermore, to host a "Great Olympics" and showcase China's strength, the Chinese people and CCP placed great emphasis on the spectacular sports venues erected for the event, such as National Stadium, as well as the opening ceremony. Ultimately, I will argue that both the Chinese historical memory of the Century of Humiliation and the political motivations of the CCP led the 2008 Beijing Olympic Games to be utilized as a spectacle to promote the image of "New China, Great Olympics," and showcase Chinese national strength on an international stage.

One day after the extravagant opening ceremonies of the 2008 Beijing Olympic Games, a euphoric statement was contained within a front-page article of a popular Chinese newspaper: "Tonight, we finally realized the hundred-year dream of [hosting] the Olympics" (as cited in Hung, 2011, p. 360). Why did the Chinese hold this hundred-year dream to host the Olympics? The answer to this query largely resides within the Chinese historical memory of the Century of Humiliation (Brownell, 2008, p. 15; deLisle, 2008, p. 26; Law, 2010, p. 349; Lau, Lam, & Leung, 2010, p. 164; Xiaobo, 2008, p. 266). The Century of Humiliation began with China's military defeat by Western imperial powers in the First Opium War of the early 1840s, which forced China to sacrifice the sovereignty of its previously guarded national borders (Askew, 2009, p. 104; Huiling, 2011, p. 168; Lau et al., 2010, pp. 162-164; Law, 2010, p. 349; Lovell, 2008, p. 762; Parker, 2008, p. 277; Xu, 2008, p. 17). In addition to this loss, the Chinese then suffered another devastating military defeat at the hands of invading Japanese forces in the 1894-1895 Sino–Japanese War, cementing China's inability to guard its national borders (Law, 2010, p. 349; Lovell, 2008, p. 162; Parker, 2008, p. 277; Xu, 2008, p. 17). This was a crucial moment in Chinese history, for these military defeats shattered the Sinocentric belief that China was the central power of the civilized world (Lovell, 2008, p. 762; Xu, 2008, p. 17). Rather, the Chinese were forced to realize that their nation was only one amongst many fighting for survival in a Western-dominated international community (Brownell, 2008, pp. 33-34; Lovell, 2008, p. 763; Xu, 2008). This belief is largely indicative of the Western concept of "Social Darwinism," developed by Thomas Henry Huxley in the 1860s, in which nations are likened to organisms that compete for resources and survival (Brownell, 2008, pp. 33-35).

The adoption of Social Darwinist thinking in China can be largely traced to the Chinese intellectual Yan Fu, who translated many Western works into Chinese including Huxley's *Education and Ethics* for an Eastern audience (Brownell, 2008, p. 55; Xu, 2008, p. 17). In 1895, Yan published a Chinese article entitled "On the origins of national strength" in which he applied the concept of Social Darwinism he encountered to the current state of the Chinese nation, which was near defeat in the Sino–Japanese war (Xu, 2008, p. 18). In this article, Yan noted that "a nation is like human. If an individual is not active physically, the body will be weak. If a person is active physically, the body will be strong" (as cited in Xu, 2008, p. 18). This statement clearly draws upon Huxley's ideas, namely that nations are like organisms, yet further establishes a direct link between the physical activity level of a nation's populace and a nation's overall strength. However, Yan then posed the following question: "does today's China look like a sick man?" (as cited in Xu, 2008, p. 18). Yan argued that China did appear as a "sick man," for its recent military woes and physical subordination to the West and Japan were signs of weakness within the international community (Xu, 2008, p. 18). Thus, it is clear overall that Yan's article established a direct link between the physical health of a nation's populace and a nation's strength as well as applied this concept to the Chinese national condition to determine that China was a "sick man."

However, this negative portrayal of China's national strength was not limited to domestic thought, as it was noted in an 1896 British journal article that China was the "Sick Man of East Asia" (Brownell, 2008, pp. 34-35; Xu, 2008, p. 19). The elites of Chinese society, ashamed at this "Sick Man" label, sought to remove this negative designation from the minds and headlines of both the Chinese and Western peoples (Askew, 2009, p. 108; Huiling, 2011, p. 121; Xiaobo, 2008, pp. 266-267). One of the most advocated methods to accomplish this goal was the adoption of Western sport because the elite class—who largely agreed with Yan Fu's connection between populace physical health and national strength—felt that Western sport could strengthen the national populace's physical condition and consequently increase China's national strength (Bridges, 2008, p. 245; Brownell, 2008, p. 49; Xu, 2008, pp. 19, 28, 61). For instance, one scholar noted that "encouraging physical training among the Chinese is essential to saving the nation" (as cited in Xu, 2008, p. 61). Another scholar stated, "the purpose for our advocating physical education and western sport focuses on removing national shame and supporting national survival and renewal" (as cited in Xu, 2008, p. 61). Yet, the best means to demonstrate China's physical strength and remove the label of the "Sick Man of East Asia" was through winning and hosting international sports competitions, goals that the Chinese thus ached to achieve (Askew, 2009, pp. 107-109; Brownell, 2008, p. 19; Law, 2010, p. 350). The desire of the Chinese to both win and host international sporting events to showcase their national strength is best demonstrated by the three "Olympic Dreams" questions (Brownell, 2008, p. 19). Posed by Chinese patriots in the Chinese YMCA program in 1907, these questions were:

> When will China be able to send a winning athlete to the Olympic contests, when will China be able to send a winning team to the Olympic contests, and when will China be able to invite all the world to Beijing for an International Olympic contest? (Brownell, 2008, p. 19)

These questions distinctly demonstrate that winning and hosting the Olympics have long been Chinese nationalistic goals to prove that they were strong (Askew, 2009, p. 104; Brownell, 2009, p. 189; Cha, 2009, pp. 64-65, 147; Hung, 2011, pp. 367, 370; Lau et al., 2010, pp. 168-169; Price, 2009, p. 5; Xu,

2008, pp. 6, 36, 267). Therefore, it is apparent that the 2008 Beijing Olympic Games were more than just a sporting event to the Chinese. Rather, they were a nationalistic spectacle to prove China's strength to the international community and shed the label that was preserved in Chinese historical memory.

This aspiration to achieve nationalistic strength was also contained within the political motivations of the CCP. The origins of these political motivations can largely be traced to the reformative ideas of Deng Xiaoping, the foremost CCP leader of the late twentieth century. Deng assumed preeminent party leadership in 1979 and immediately established a new direction for CCP rule (Brady, 2009, p. 4). Under the previous leadership of Mao Zedong, the CCP garnered its ruling legitimacy from revolutionary communist ideologies that offered an alternative to Western capitalism (Askew, 2009, p. 106). In contrast, Deng sought to recast the CCP as a "party in power" rather than as a "revolutionary party" (Askew, 2009, p. 106). As part of this recasting, Deng orchestrated a shift in the CCP's economic ideology from communism to "socialism with Chinese characteristics" (Askew, 2009, p. 106), which involved a series of market reform and opening-up policies. Due to these market liberalizing policies, the CCP could no longer rely upon revolutionary communist ideology to establish legitimacy and thus sought to fill this ideological vacuum through a variety of alternative principles (Brownell, 2008, pp. 63-64; Haugen, 2008, p. 146; Xu, 2008, pp. 198, 202). Of these alternative principles, one of the most imperative was an increased sense of Chinese popular nationalism (Askew, 2009, p. 106; Brady, 2009, p. 3; Brownell, 2009, pp. 63-64; Haugen, 2008, p. 146).

One of the most visible ways in which the CCP attempted to generate this popular nationalism was through success in international sport, since this would create an image of a strong China and subsequently increase CCP legitimacy (Brady, 2009, p. 3; Law, 2010, p. 353; Jarvie, Hwang, & Brennan, 2008, p. 99; Xiaobo, 2008, p. 267). Efforts to utilize international sport and the Olympic Games in this manner began as early as 1979, when the Chinese National Sports Commission developed an "Olympic Model" for winning certain events at the 1980 Olympic Games (Xu, 2008, p. 197). The CCP's use of international sport to showcase China's strength was once again demonstrated at the 1984 Olympic Games, at which CCP representatives openly linked success in sports competitions with national honor and prestige (Xu, 2008, p. 202). Furthermore, the 15 gold medals won by Chinese athletes at the 1984 Olympics—the first such medals in Chinese history—were portrayed by the CCP as "just the beginning" for the Chinese who sought to prove their nation's strength (Brady, 2009, p. 3; deLisle, 2008, p. 25; Jarvie et al., 2008, p. 99; Xiaobo, 2008, p. 264; Xu, 2008, p. 203). Finally, scholars have readily noted that no other country or government has been as eager to increase its international prestige through international sporting events as China and the CCP (Askew, 2009, pp. 109, 114; Brady, 2009, pp. 5,7; Dong-Jhy, Barnier, Heitzman, & Wei-Cheng, 2011, p. 119; Hung, 2011; Tong, 2008, pp. 249-250; Xiaobo, 2008, p. 265; Xu, 2008, p. 203). Therefore, it is once again clear that the 2008 Beijing Olympic Games were more than merely a sporting event. Rather, the CCP utilized the Games as a spectacle to showcase Chinese national strength in order to generate popular nationalism for its own legitimacy.

The clearest and most succinct manifestation of these nationalistic intentions is contained within the official, international slogan of the Beijing Games: "New China, Great Olympics" (Law, 2010, p. 350; Xu, 2008, p. 243). The "New China" represented in this slogan was a revitalized nation, whose populace sought to portray their selection as host of the 2008 Olympics as a sign that China had recovered from the Century of Humiliation (Law, 2010, p. 350; Xu, 2008, p. 243). Furthermore, the Chinese wanted to utilize their position as host to symbolically reestablish China's national strength in the international community and prove to Olympic visitors that China could compete with the western powers (Law, 2010, p. 350; Xu, 2008, p. 243). In the attempt to grandly showcase the "New China's" regained strength to the visiting athletes and spectators of the Beijing Games, the Chinese instituted a series of reforms between the 2001 announcement and the 2008 Games. One such reform was the modernization of Beijing's uninspiring transportation infrastructure (Cha, 2009, pp. 111-113; Bridges, 2011, p. 246; Hung, 2011, p. 360; Jinxia, 2011, p. 169). It is estimated that the Chinese spent 40 billion U.S. dollars on this reform effort, the most ever spent on infrastructure develop-

ments for an Olympic event (Cha, 2009, pp. 111-113; Bridges, 2011, p. 246; Hung, 2011, p. 360; Jinxia, 2011, p. 169). While this budget was widely distributed on a number of projects, including the creation of new expressways and four new subway lines, one of the most expensive aspects of this effort was the construction of Terminal 3 at Beijing International Airport (Cha, 2009, p. 111). At the time it was built, Terminal 3 was the largest airport terminal in the world and it was meant to demonstrate China's strength to Olympic visitors immediately upon their entry to the "New China" (Cha, 2009, pp. 111-112). Thus, the modernization of Beijing's infrastructure was clearly a manifestation of the desire to showcase China's national strength to Olympic visitors.

Another reform movement undertaken between 2001 and 2008 was a campaign aimed toward improving the manners of Chinese citizens (Brady, 2009, pp.17-18; Cha, 2009, p. 70; deLisle, 2008, pp. 24-25; Law, 2010, pp.351-352; Xu, 2008, pp 251-252). This campaign sought to reform a number of civilian habits that the Chinese feared would be negatively viewed by Olympic tourists, such as cutting in line, spitting in public and littering (Brady, 2009, pp.17-18; Cha, 2009, p. 70; deLisle, 2008, pp. 24-25; Law, 2010, pp. 351-352; Xu, 2008, pp 251-252). The good host campaign was instituted directly by the Communist Party-state apparatus as evidenced by the inclusion of high-ranking members of the Communist Party on the Beijing Organizing Committee for the Olympic Games (BOCOG). Overall, BOCOG had 650 Communist Party members who led the good host campaign from a top-down perspective. The programs themselves were instituted through targeted school programs and the distribution of Olympic readers that espoused the manners that the Chinese government wanted their citizens to demonstrate (Law, 2010, pp. 343-367). Ultimately, this campaign was clearly an attempt to showcase the strength of the "New China" to Olympic visitors through the projection of a strong, civilized national populace (Cha, 2009, p. 71).

China properly demonstrated this through not only reforming their infrastructure and manners, but also improve their performance in the Olympic sporting events themselves. The desire to utilize the Olympic sporting events as a platform to demonstrate China's strength was directly related to the shame of the Century of Humiliation and the ideas of Yan Fu, as the modern Chinese still linked the physical ability of a nation's populace with national strength (Hung, 2011, p. 360; Law, 2010, p. 350; Xu, 2008, p. 267). This link was clearly reestablished in an article of the *The People's Daily* that was published following the 2004 Athens Olympics (Lovell, 2008, pp. 773). This article noted that "when a country is powerful, its sports will flourish… Chinese athletes will make contributions to realize our nation's great revival" (as cited in Lovell, 2008, pp. 773). Thus, in order to strengthen the performance of Chinese athletes and consequently showcase a strong nation, the "Plan to Win Glory in the 2008 Olympics" was implemented in 2002 (Lau et al., 2011, p. 163). This plan identified 119 gold medals that the Chinese sought to win in events such as swimming and gymnastics, increased the budget for these athletics teams and created a new nutrition plan for these athletes that would allot them a higher calorie intake (Brady, 2009, p. 7; Lau et al., 2011, p. 163). Although Chinese athletes did not win all 119 medals identified in this plan, China still topped the medal count with 51 gold medals, 15 more than the second-place finisher (Brady, 2009, p. 7; Huiling, 2011, pp. 102, 275; Xu, 2008, p. 268). These athletic victories were seen as a great source of Chinese national pride, as it showcased to the world that China no longer deserved the "Sick Man of East Asia" label (Askew, 2008, p. 110; Brady, 2009, p. 7; Cha, 2009, pp. 3, 66; Xu, 2008, p. 257). Therefore, the athletic accomplishments of Chinese Olympians can ultimately be seen as another attempt to demonstrate the "New China's" strength to the world, since athletic success was promoted in order to project the image of a strong China to the international community. Overall, it is clear that the modernization of Beijing's infrastructure, the reform of the populace's manners and the success of Chinese athletes were all Chinese attempts to showcase the "New China's" national strength on the international stage of the Olympics.

However, the Chinese did not only wish to showcase their national strength through their modern infrastructure, polite populace and accomplished athletes. Rather, they further desired to showcase their national strength through their ability to host a "Great Olympics" (Law, 2010, p. 350; Xu, 2008, p. 243). The ability to smoothly host countries from all over the world at the preeminent international sporting event was seen as a great source of nationalistic pride for the Chinese, as it was an enormous event that required meticulous planning and coordination (Cha, 2009, pp. 36, 61; deLisle, 2008, p. 32; Lau et al., 2011, p. 169; Lovell, 2008, p. 767). Yet, the Chinese further sought to utilize their position as host to showcase their national strength by providing the "most dazzling chapter yet in Olympic history" (Lovell, 2008, p. 767). To host this "Great Olympics" and demonstrate China's strength, the Chinese emphasized the creation of spectacular sports venues and a grand performance at the Games opening ceremony (Lovell, 2008, p. 767). The most notable sports venue and iconic symbol of the 2008 Beijing Games was National Stadium, which is more commonly referred to as the Bird's Nest due to its weaved steel frame that encloses the inner-arena (Cha, 2009, p. 112; Hung, 2011, p. 360). This unorthodox design was the creation of Swiss architect Jacques Herzog, who noted that "you couldn't do such an avant-garde structure anywhere else, but the Chinese are so fresh in mind…everyone is encouraged to do their most stupid and extravagant designs there. National Stadium tells me nothing will shake them" (Xu, 2008, p. 254). This statement clearly indicates that the daring to attempt such a complex design project and the ability to successfully complete its construction were meant to be a sign of Chinese strength in the international community. Therefore, the spectacular venues of the 2008 Olympics were clearly a method for China host a "Great Olympics" and thereby showcase its national strength to the world.

The extravagant opening ceremony of the 2008 Beijing Olympic Games was another method by which the Chinese sought to demonstrate their strength and ability to host the international community. The opening ceremony is a crucial event for all Olympic hosts, since it allows nations to fashion a narrative of their country that is broadcasted internationally to large audiences (Barmé, 2009, p. 67; Brownell, 2008, p. 165; Kennett & de Moragas, 2008, p. 262). Due to its ability to craft and project a narrative, including one of national strength, the opening ceremony was assigned a high-level of importance by the CCP (Barmé, 2009, p. 64; Brady, 2009, pp. 19-20; Hung, 2011, p. 360). The CCP's emphasis on the opening ceremony is clearly demonstrated by its strict guidelines for the event, which stated that the ceremony should be "outstanding, innovative...[reflecting] the strong spirit of the age" (Barmé, 2009, p. 70). Furthermore, the CCP hoped to "take an international perspective," as well as highlight the "brilliant civilization" of the Qing era and the "glorious era" of the modern day (Barmé, 2009, p. 70). Thus, the principal goal of the organizers and choreographers of the opening ceremony was to grandly and spectacularly showcase China's historical journey as a strong nation, highlighting China's traditional and renewed strength, while notably omitting signs of weakness like the Century of Humiliation (Barmé, 2009, p. 68; Hung, 2011, p. 363). Within themselves, these guidelines for the opening ceremony clearly demonstrate that the ceremony was a method for China to host a "Great Olympics" as well as showcase its strength to the international community.

Yet, the Chinese did not only seek to demonstrate national strength and host a "Great Olympics" through the narrative of the opening ceremony, but also through the organized and disciplined nature of the actors as well. This is most clearly demonstrated in the initial act of the event that opened with 2,008 stylized drummers playing traditional *fou* drums in near-perfect unison, demonstrating an outstanding ability to organize a grand event (Barmé, 2009, p. 71; Hung, 2011, p. 366). Furthermore, over 14,000 actors participated in the opening ceremony that was executed flawlessly, once again demonstrating the ability of the Chinese to carefully coordinate this spectacular event (Brady, 2009, p. 19; Hung, 2011, pp. 364, 367). Therefore, it is clear that the CCP sought to utilize the narrative and coordination of the Beijing Games' opening ceremony as another opportunity to host a "Great Olympics" and thereby demonstrate China's strength and ability to host the international community. Overall, both the spectacular venues and the opening ceremony of the 2008 Beijing Olympic Games were clearly meant to showcase China's national strength through its ability to host a "Great Olympics."

In conclusion, it is clear that the Chinese treated the 2008 Beijing Olympic Games as more than a mere international sporting event, as they were utilized as a spectacle to reestablish China's strength on the international stage. The use of the Beijing Games in this manner was largely grounded in both Chinese his-

torical memory and CCP political motivations. The shattered Sino-centric worldview led the Chinese to realize that their nation was only one amongst many fighting for survival. This Eastern application of Social Darwinism was strongly advocated by the Chinese intellectual Yan Fu created a direct connection for the Chinese between a physically strong populace and a strong nation, leading many Chinese elites to advocate the adoption of Western sport to prove that their country was no longer the "Sick Man of East Asia." To prove this to themselves and the rest of the world, the Chinese long sought to both win and host international sporting events. Consequently, it is clear that the Chinese truly utilized the 2008 Beijing Olympic Games as a spectacle to showcase China's national strength in order to prove that it is no longer the "Sick Man of East Asia."

Furthermore, the desire to showcase China's national strength on the international stage of the 2008 Olympics was also contained within the political motivations of the CCP. Due to Deng Xiaoping's shift of party ideology, the CCP could no longer rely upon Maoist doctrines for its ruling legitimacy. Instead, the CCP sought to establish its legitimacy through a variety of factors, including an increased sense of popular nationalism. One of the most important means by which this nationalism could be generated was through strong Chinese performances in international sport. These strong performances would portray the image of a strong China to the international community and subsequently increase popular nationalism and CCP legitimacy. Therefore, it is clear that the CCP also sought to utilize the 2008 Beijing Olympic Games as a spectacle to promote China's national strength in order to satisfy its own political goal of generating popular nationalism. These two nationalistic desires to promote China's regained strength on the international stage were most clearly manifested in the 2008 Beijing Olympic Games through the official slogan of "New China, Great Olympics." To showcase a "New China" to Olympic visitors, the Chinese modernized Beijing's transportation infrastructure, promoted mass campaigns to reform the manners of its citizens, and sought to dominate on the sports field to top the medal count. Similarly, to host a "Great Olympics" and thus further demonstrate China's national strength to the international community, the Chinese people and the

CCP placed great emphasis on the spectacular sports venues erected for the event, such as the Bird's Nest Stadium, and the opening ceremony, which was centered on a narrative of national strength. Ultimately, it is clearly proven that both the Chinese historical memory of the Century of Humiliation and the political motivations of the CCP led the 2008 Beijing Olympic Games to be utilized as a spectacle to promote the image of "New China, Great Olympics," and showcase Chinese national strength on an international stage.

REFERENCES

Askew, D. (2009). Sports and politics: The 2008 Beijing olympic games. *European Studies: A Journal of European Culture, History and Politics, 27*(October), 103-120. doi:10.1163/9789042027428_008

Barmé, G. R. (2009). China's flat earth: History and 8 August 2008. *The China Quarterly, 197*(March), 64-86. doi:10.1017/S0305741009000046

Brady, A. (2009). The Beijing Olympics as a campaign of mass distraction. *The China Quarterly, 197*(March), 1-24. doi:10.1017/S0305741009000058

Bridges, B. (2011). Beyond the Olympics: Power, change and legacy. *The International Journal of China Studies, 2*(2), 243-257.

Brownell, S. (2008). *Beijing's Games: What the Olympics mean to China.* New York, NY: Rowman and Littlefield.

Brownell, S. (2009). Beijing's Olympic education programme: Re-thinking Suzhi education, re-imagining an international China. *The China Quarterly, 197*(March), 44-63. doi:10.1017/S0305741009000034

Cha, V. D. (2009). *Beyond the final score: The politics of sport in Asia.* New York, NY: Columbia University Press.

deLisle, J. (2008). One world, different dreams: The contest to define the Beijing Olympics. In M. E. Price & D. Dayan (Eds.), *Owning the Olympics: Narratives of the new China* (pp. 17-66). Ann Arbor, MI: University of Michigan Press.

Dong-Jhy, H., Bairner, A., Heitzmen, K., & Wei-Cheng, C. (2011). Sport, national identity, and Taiwan's Olympic history. In W. W Kelly & S. Brownell (Eds.), *The Olympics in East Asia: Nationalism, regionalism, and globalism on the center stage of world sports* (pp. 119-146). New Haven, CT: Yale University Council on East Asian Studies.

Haugen, H. O. (2008). A very natural choice: The construction of Beijing as an Olympic city during the bid period. In M. E. Price & D. Dayan (Eds.), *Owning the Olympics: Narratives of the new China* (pp. 145-162). Ann Arbor, MI: University of Michigan Press.

Huiling, F. (2011). *The humanistic values of the Beijing Olympics.* Singapore: Silkroad Press.

Hung, C. (2011). The politics of national celebrations in China. In W. C. Kirby (Ed.), *The People's Republic of China at 60: An international assessment* (pp. 357-372). Cambridge, MA: Harvard University Press.

Jarvie, G., Hwang, D., & Brennan, M. (2008). *Sport, Revolution and the Beijing Olympics.* New York, NY: Berg Publishers.

Jinxia, D. (2011). National identity, Olympics victory, and Chinese sportswomen in the global era. In W. W Kelly & S. Brownell (Eds.), *The Olympics in East Asia: nationalism, regionalism, and globalism on the center stage of world sports* (pp. 161-184). New Haven, CT: Yale University Council on East Asian Studies.

Kennett, C., & de Moragas, M., (2008). From Athens to Beijing: The closing ceremony and Olympic television broadcast narrative. In M. E. Price & D. Dayan (Eds.), *Owning the Olympics: Narratives of the new China* (pp. 260-282). Ann Arbor, MI: University of Michigan Press.

60

Lau, P., Lam, M., & Leung, B. (2011). The Beijing Olympics and expressions of national identity in China, Taiwan and Hong Kong. In W. W. Kelly & S. Brownell (Eds.), *The Olympics in East Asia: Nationalism, regionalism, and globalism on the center stage of world sports* (pp. 147-160). New Haven, CT: Yale University Council on East Asian Studies.

Law, W. (2010). The state, citizenship education, and international events in a global age: The 2008 Beijing Olympic games. *Comparative Education Review, 54*(3), 343-367. doi:10.1086/649425

Lovell, J. (2008). Prologue: Beijing 2008 - the mixed messages of contemporary Chinese nationalism. *The International Journal of the History of Sport, 25*(7), 758-778. doi:10.1080/09523360802009131

Parker, E. (2008). Dragons win: The Beijing games and Chinese nationalism. In M. Worden (Ed.), *China's great leap: The Beijing games and Olympian human rights challenges*, pp. 273-282. New York, NY: Seven Stories Press.

Price, M. E. (2009). Introduction. In Price, M. E., & Dayan, D., (Eds.), *Owning the olympics: Narratives of the new China* (pp. 1-13). Ann Arbor, MI: University of Michigan Press.

Tong, B. (2008). Modern games, old Chinese communist party. In M. Worden (Ed.), *China's great leap: The Beijing games and Olympian human rights challenges* (pp. 249-253). New York, NY: Seven Stories Press.

Xiaobo, L. (2008). Authoritarianism in the light of the Olympic flame. In M. Worden (Ed.), *China's great leap: The Beijing games and Olympian human rights challenges* (pp. 263-272). New York, NY: Seven Stories Press.

Xu, G. (2008). *Olympic dreams: China and sports, 1895-2008*. Cambridge, MA: Harvard University Press.

Fist of Fury or *Drunken Master*: Masculinity, National Identity, and Contemporary China

Peter Benson

ABSTRACT

Despite being products of the same historical moment in Chinese culture, Bruce Lee and Jackie Chan approached the kung fu genre with radically different methods that effectually developed two contrasting kung fu identities: that of tragedy, and that of comedy, respectively. Lee and Chan's embracement of these distinct kung fu identities helped them to engage with transnational issues in Chinese history in ways that were easily accessible to global audiences. While Bruce Lee's films present Lee as a victor who successfully resists the imperial oppression that victimized China during the Century of Humiliation,* Jackie Chan's represent 21st century China's rise to power on the international stage. In this paper, I argue that the films of Bruce Lee and Jackie Chan can be deployed as a lens to demonstrate their engagement with the fluidity and evolution of the masculinity and national identity of the Chinese people.

Bruce Lee and Jackie Chan are two of the most legendary and influential figures in the history of Chinese cinema. Lee and Chan approached the kung fu genre by utilizing radically different methods; these methods effectually developed two contrasting kung fu identities: tragedy and comedy. Lee and Chan's embracement of these distinct kung fu identities helped them engage in China's history of transnational issues in ways that were easily accessible to global audiences. Specifically, Lee deployed the use of racial politics in his films through the advocation of a Chinese national identity, and utilized his own body as a focal point to alter existing Chinese stereotypes by reinventing Chinese masculinity as resilient, powerful, and competitive. While the iconic Chairman Mao helped China confront the pains of the Century of Humilation through politics and economics, Lee's films served as a form of catharsis for the national identity and masculinity of the disgraced Chinese people (Rowman & Littlefield, 2007). Just

as Mao's death led to the birth of a new China, it can be argued that Lee's death created a void in the genre that Lee's successor, Jackie Chan, refused to be molded by. Instead, by transforming kung fu tragedy into kung fu comedy, Chan generated a new wave of kung fu cinema that drastically altered the attitude of the medium, and consequently challenged Lee's portrayal of toughness. In contrast to Lee's hard-bodied image, Chan's utilization of humor and comedy returned humanity to the cold masculinity of Lee. This widened the appeal of the kung fu genre beyond the growing pains of the Chinese to the middle class on a global scale. While Bruce Lee's films present Lee as a victor who successfully resists the imperial oppression that victimized China during the Century of Humiliation, Jackie Chan's represent 21st century China's rise to power on the international stage. It can be argued that the films of Bruce Lee and Jackie Chan can be deployed as a lens to demonstrate their engagement with the fluidity and evolution of the

---

*The "Century of Humiliation" is a term used to describe a period that started in 1840 and ended in 1949 when Mao came to power. This period was characterized by a decrease in China's autonomy due to the expansion of foreign imperial powers such as Japan and Great Britain. According to historian Peter Hays Gries, the century of humiliation consists of two simultaneous narratives for the Chinese people, that of the victor and that of the victim. He discusses this extensively in his article "Narratives to live by: The Century of Humiliation and the Chinese National Identity Today." See Peter Hays Gries, *China's Transformations: The Stories Beyond the Headlines*, 2007.

masculinity and national identity of the Chinese people.

In order to assess the perceptions of Chinese masculinity and national identity possessed by Lee and Chan, one must first understand the historical context in which they operated and the humiliation that they attempted to overcome. Bruce Lee was born in 1940, at the end of China's Century of Humiliation that spanned from 1840 to 1949. This period represents China's loss of territory and control of their region to imperialist powers. The Century of Humiliation emerged in the wake of the first Opium War in which a series of treaties would result in China losing Hong Kong to Great Britain and being forced to pay punishing indemnities to compensate colonial powers for its losses. These treaties were known as the "Unequal Treaties" because Britain had no obligations despite the amount China was forced to give up. The treaties represented the shift in the balance of power from China to the colonial state (Kaufman, 2010).

China also faced degradation from their eastern rival Japan, who had recognized the utility of western power and influence prior to their fellow easterners, and utilized it to annex Korea and Taiwan in 1910 and 1895 respectively. These acts contributed an additional devastating blow to China's regional influence. As the power of China declined, its government was targeted by various revolutionary movements, resulting in the fall of the Qing dynasty and rise of the Republic of China in 1912. However, this government still suffered from a lack of public support and geographical unification resulting in further harassment from the opportunistic Japanese, most notably during the second Sino–Japanese War (Wilson, 1982).

The most notable memory of the Sino–Japanese war for the Chinese was the infamous Nanking Massacre, also known as the "Rape of Nanking," in which 200,000 to 300,000 Chinese civilians were murdered by Japanese soldiers (Chang, 1997). Despite China appearing as Japan's main adversary during the war, in reality, China was propped up by German, American, and Soviet funding essentially making China a pawn in a game between imperial power players. Though it received economic aid, China still struggled to fend off Japanese aggression until the

United States eventually dropped atomic bombs on Nagasaki and Hiroshima in order to end the Second World War. Despite being a victor of World War II, the Chinese people had grown increasingly agitated after nearly a century of foreign oppression resulting in a post-war political and economic collapse, allowing Mao Zedong and his regime to rise to power and subsequently announce that the Century of Humiliation was at an end.

Figure 1. "Paratrooper manoeuvres," (CPC/1/J/18). Courtesy of The University of Westminster Archive

The events of the Century of Humiliation drastically altered the Chinese people's understanding of their own national identity. For men in particular, every abuse from foreign imperial powers against China as a nation also symbolically stripped the individual of their own sense of masculinity. Exploring this concept, that Chinese national identity and masculinity are linked such that the role, or identity, of China on the international stage must be understood through its own perception of gender roles.

In her writing about the Chinese's understanding of gender during the Qing dynasty, historian Janet M. Theiss states, "The normative significance of chastity [is] disproportionately amplified by the concrete social and political value of female virtue as an aspect of…reputation" (as cited in Brownell & Wasserstrom, 2002, p. 48). This concept, despite having to do with femininity rather than masculinity, is applicable to the violation of China's national identity when it is repeatedly, literally, and figuratively violated by the brutal influence of imperial nations. Meanwhile, these powers became the masculine partner in their relationship with China, placing them in an emasculated effeminate role.

For the Chinese, "illicit sexual intercourse represented an assault on the patriarchal household. Specifically, that assault was envisioned as being made by an outside male on another man's household" (Brownell & Wasserstrom, 2002, p. 69). Therefore, at the end of the Century of Humiliation, China's national identity consisted of the disgraced female, raped of her virtue and chastity by imperial powers, and the helpless male, who had failed to protect his household, a physical manifestation of his masculinity.

The way China traditionally categorizes gender roles further complicates the dilemma of their national identity. For westerners, gender is typically seen as a product of primary sex characteristics, but the Chinese believe that the way one acts and behaves is more insightful towards their gender identity (Brownell & Wasserstrom, 2002). Therefore, Chinese males were unable to look between their legs to reinforce their sense of masculinity, and instead had to assess their gender by reflecting on their actions, which, as stated earlier, would have been an incredibly humbling task following the Century of Humiliation. Due to China's self-perceived humiliation and masculine deficiencies, a space emerged for Mao Zedong and Bruce Lee to end the Century of Humiliation and return masculinity to the Chinese people.

To combat the victim image of China as a raped female during the Century of Humiliation, Mao stressed the heroic victories of the Chinese people against imperial powers. Gries (2007) states:

> Under Mao, China's modern sufferings were blamed on the feudalism of the Qing dynasty and Western imperialism, and the Maoist account of the century highlighted the heroism of the anti-feudal, anti-imperialist masses in throwing-off their chains and repelling foreign invaders. (p. 116)

From this, Mao was able to reimagine the experience of the Chinese people during the Century of Hu-

milation as resilient, perseverant, and heroic rather submissive and struggling. This transformation of a victim narrative into a victor narrative is indicative of the "fist of fury" that Lee would later utilize to bring national pride and masculinity back to the Chinese people.

In order to successfully manipulate the understanding of the Century of Humiliation and simultaneously cultivate pride for the Chinese Communist Party, Mao suppressed any writing that utilized the symbol of China as a raped woman (Gries, 2007). In its place emerged media regaling the bravery and masculinity of heroes, such as Lin Zexu, in their rebellion against foreign invaders as a rallying cry for the nation (Gries, 2007). Mao continued the effort of reinventing China's nationality and masculinity through a victor narrative throughout his career ultimately culminating in his sponsorship of the Great Proletarian Cultural Revolution in August of 1966 (Schoppa, 2011).

Several Cultural Revolution posters hailed Chinese men, particularly those who were physically strong, as cultural heroes. Many of these posters featured men who were physically robust and were often depicted as having a background in the military or engaging in physically demanding labor. These posters celebrated the work ethic and tenacity of the prole-

Figure 2. "Women can hold up half the sky; surely the face of nature can be transformed," (CPC/1/Q/1). Courtesy of The University of Westminster Archive

tariat in addition to demonstrating the technological advances China had made in industry, military, and agriculture. Posters that depict females (who are not in the context of a man or simply studying Mao's philosophies) portrayed them as having masculine features, wearing masculine clothes, and engaging in physical labor. This celebration of ideal male characteristics in both men *and* women during one of China's most important revolutions highlights their strong cultural bond between masculinity and national identity.

Like Mao, Bruce Lee engaged with the victor narrative and utilized similar tactics to highlight the heroism of anti-imperialists. Throughout his entire filmography, Lee continually placed the national honor of the Chinese at stake by villainizing the Japanese, or conjured the history of contemporary Chinese colonialism by villainizing British imperials. According to his widow:

> Bruce's whole life [is] a play between East and West. He hated the oppression of "little people," which he saw everywhere: in the Japanese occupations, the Boxer Rebellion, the foreign powers going into China, he…thought all of that was wrong. (sia gunn, 2014)

In essence, both Lee and Mao took the victim narrative of the Century of Humiliation and upturned it into a heroic victor narrative. Because he worked in a historical moment after China had been repeatedly disgraced and violated by foreign powers, Lee's cinematic triumphs acted as therapy to anyone in the act of reconfiguring their own cultural identity. Therefore, Lee became a champion to any Chinese person who had felt the oppression of colonial powers and successfully turned the victor narrative of the Century of Humiliation into a victor narrative.

Several common themes throughout Lee's films allowed him to act as a vessel for his own national identity, while also avoiding the alienation of his culturally diverse audience. Lee acted as a champion of the Chinese people. In films such as *The Big Boss* and *Way of the Dragon*, Lee leaves his ancestral homeland to aid expatriate Chinese who are living in oppression by foreigners. This strong commitment to family and a sense of national identity in a culturally for-

eign land resonated with third world audiences and migrant workers who were experiencing the same experiences of alienation. Additionally, the wardrobe of powerful figures in Lee's films, including Lee himself, typically consists of clothing traditional to mainland China (Chow & Wei, 1971). For example, in *Fist of Fury*, Lee sports a *Zhongshan* suit, which had grown in popularity among Chinese men because of Mao Zedong's fondness towards them starting in 1949. Conversely, Lee's Japanese adversaries wear traditional Japanese clothing, including *kategis*. This careful wardrobe selection polarizes, racializes, and radicalizes the conflict to audiences. The hero, Lee, was visually Chinese, and the villains were visually Japanese therefore thrusting the Chinese national identity in the face of foreign adversaries.

Figure 3. "Reap a big harvest and store grain everywhere," (CPC/1/A/60). Courtesy of The University of Westminster Archive

Lee's most legendary fight scene is an excellent example of this concept. In *Fist of Fury*, Japanese samurai question the strength and masculinity of the members of a Chinese martial arts school by sending them a banner inscribed "Sick Men of Asia" (Chow & Wei, 1972). This is a direct assault against both the Chinese national identity and the masculine body. Upon being presented the banner, Lee remains passive, seething in anger but also demonstrating level-headedness in the face of humiliation. This patience is later rewarded when Lee visits the Japanese dojo with banner in hand (thus branding the Japanese as "sick men") (Chow & Wei, 1972). He then proceeds to defeat the entire class and its instructor single-handedly before stating, "Now you listen to me…We are not sick men!" (Chow & Wei, 1972). By utilizing the word "we," Lee places the model of Chinese national identity and masculinity upon his own shoulders (Shu, 2004, p. 50). During the fight itself, Lee removes his shirt, drawing focus to his muscular body, which stands in contrast to the robed Japanese. Additionally, Lee picks up two Japanese combatants and whirls like a dervish before launching them across the room. If the 5'7" Bruce Lee, who weighed in at only 128 pounds, could man-handle two Japanese men in such a way, surely other Chinese men could do the same (Shu, 2003, p. 50).

The subservient role of women in Lee's films also strengthens Lee's own masculine image. Throughout his filmography, Lee drinks, has sex, and has frequent rendezvous with prostitutes (Chow & Wei, 1971). In *The Big Boss*, Lee gets drunk, impressing his friends, and then is "seduced" by a prostitute (Chow & Wei, 1971). Lee's domination of the female's contrasting femininity portrays Lee as a "man's man" with sex appeal, all of which reinforce his own masculine image, and therefore the Chinese national identity.

Figure 4. "Develop military sports activities and defend the socialist motherland," (CPC/1/J/27). Courtesy of The University of Westminster Archive

Understanding the effectiveness of Lee's utilization of the kung fu genre requires an exploration of the historical birth of the genre. By doing this, we can gain insight on why kung fu films were an effective medium and how they relate to China's national identity. Contrary to popular belief, the use of martial arts in Chinese cinema extends beyond just kung fu films. *Wuxia*, which translates to English as "martial hero," is a wide genre of Chinese fiction concerning the story of a martial artist in ancient China (Teo, 2009). Despite being over 2,000 years old, the modern wuxia did not emerge into popularity until 1920.

The genre's modern growth was a result of the May Fourth Movement, which urged the Chinese people to value movies and literature that broke away from traditional Confucian values. Like the Chinese national hoped to do during the May Fourth Movement, the protagonist, or *xia*, of the wuxia genre became a symbol of freedom in defiance of tradition. As a result of its sudden relevance in modern culture, the wuxia medium and its popularity continued to grow. The popular genre subsequently developed subgenres, one of which was the *shenguai wuxia* (martial arts of ghosts and spirits) subgenre (Teo, 2009). Shenguai wuxia featured heavy usage of special effects and fantasy tropes that ended up turning off viewers to the film, rather than sparking their imaginations. As a reactionary backlash to the shenguai subgenre, kung fu films were developed after 1938. While kung fu films still feature a xia-like character, the genre utilized heavy realism, martial arts, and a contemporary setting, all of which stood in stark contrast to typical wuxia tropes. This realistic and modern setting served as the perfect backdrop, allowing Bruce Lee (and later Jackie Chan) to effectively shatter the silver screen and send a direct message to their respective audiences.

In addition to being realistic, kung fu films had the advantage of being relatively straightforward in plot. They were therefore able to portray a more abstract message, as the audience did not have to mentally process and interpret the proceedings of the film before analyzing its message. The focus of the film shifted instead to the characters who drove the actions, but, uniquely, the characters remained simple and served only to highlight Bruce Lee as the central point of the film. The names and backstories of the characters may have shifted from film to film, but Lee essentially played himself in all of his movies. This explains the success of the genre despite its shallowness: audiences were magnetized by the raw talent of Lee rather than intricate plots, interesting characters, or witty dialogue. In his films, Lee was not a Chinese man playing characters; he was simply a Chinese man being himself. Even timeless characters such as Chen Zhen, originally portrayed by Lee and later resurrected by Donnie Yen and Jet Li, are merely reflections of Lee. By allowing Chinese men to be themselves rather than attempting to portray a character, the simplistic realism of the kung fu genre placed Chinese masculinity and physical prowess at the forefront.

Despite the effectiveness of Lee's films for conveying his ideologies, they also have limitations. Clearly, Lee had improved China's perception of its own masculinity and national identity; nevertheless, he was unable to extend his reach past his own anti-imperial sentiments. While Lee presented himself as the hero of the victor narrative in the face of oppression, his reliance on the victim/victor narrative as a backdrop perpetuated China's subservience at the international level. Furthermore, while China certainly had a variety of heroes during its Century of Humiliation, it is inarguable that these heroes are a minority and an exception to the suffering and tragedy endured by masses of Chinese people. The need for Lee and Mao's victim narrative only served to allow those not ready to confront the trauma to ignore their fears rather than overcome them. Toward the time of his death, Lee's caricature of hypermasculinity, treatment of women, and racial preoccupations no longer reflected the views of the global world around him. If the Chinese wanted to maintain the development of their national identity on a global scale into the late 20th and 21st centuries, the kung fu genre needed to evolve. The death of Bruce Lee created a void in the genre within which Lee's successor, Jackie Chan, refused to continue. Instead, by infusing the kung fu genre with comedy, Chan generated a new wave of kung fu cinema that drastically altered the attitude of and towards the medium.

China itself also underwent a massive shift in ideology under Deng Xiaoping. "Socialism with Chinese Characteristics" would allow China to shed the skin of prior economic failures and become included in transnational neoliberal capitalism on their own terms (Schoppa, 2011, p. 367). The People's Republic of China (PRC) government maintains to this day that it has not abandoned Marxism, but is simply redefining many of the aspects of Marxist theory to accommodate its new economic system. Similarly, Jackie Chan had to reimagine the kung fu genre in order to broaden the appeal beyond victims of oppression by instead marketing himself to a massive global middle-class audience that was dominated by western culture.

Chan's first films unsuccessfully attempted to fit the mold first pioneered by Lee (Shu, 2003). Chan was talented but was no replacement for the iconic Chinese hero. To solve this dilemma, Jackie Chan needed to change the kung fu genre and create his own mold. Once he gained creative control, he set out to (literally) change the face of kung fu cinema. To do this, Chan became the antithesis to Lee: "When he kicks high, I kick low. When he [is] not smiling, I [am] always smiling. He can [take] one-punch [to] break the wall; after I break the wall, I hurt. [After that] I do the funny face" (Shu, 2003, p. 50).

Chan adapted the kung fu genre to appeal beyond victims of oppression by marketing himself to a global middle-class audience. By abandoning China's victim narrative, Chan dissipated the threat of modern China seeking revenge on their imperial oppressors. Furthermore, in contrast to the cold, hardened masculinity Lee and Mao tied to China's national identity, Chan instead emphasized globality, hybridity, and circulation. Like Lee, Chan's earlier films typically featured a Chinese man in Asia, but, in his American cinema debut, *Rumble in the Bronx*, Chan is instead a Chinese man in New York City. Rather than providing western audiences with a window into Eastern culture, Chan shatters the fourth wall by placing himself in a middle-class western society. Chan's desire to return humanity to the Chinese kung fu star led to his great success in the genre.

Just as China needed to shed the skin of Mao to progress, Chan would need to uproot everything Lee had established in the genre to make it his own. In contrast to Lee's visibly Chinese wardrobe, Chan's American films featured him wearing jean jackets, boxer briefs, t-shirts, and light wash jeans, further demonstrating to the western audience that he could successfully adopt their culture. Lee's choice to wear Mao's suggested garment of choice in his films personified China, but had the drawback of portraying it through a figure who represented communism and other alienating concepts to the western world. Outside of Chan's wardrobe, the outfits worn by characters in *Rumble in the Bronx* highlight (in an almost corny way) New York City's own diversity with characters personifying punk, Native American, gangster, greaser, and a variety of other aesthetics. Therefore, Chan and his films advocate the expression of hybridity, plurality, and global circulation. Through this careful wardrobe selection, Jackie Chan cemented himself as a homogenous part of western society.

Instead of racial politics fueling his films, Chan further differentiated himself from Lee by making racial diversity comical. Chan himself faced a variety of humorous growing pains as a Chinese man in the western world. For example, in *Rumble in the Bronx*, Chan believes the first Asian woman he sees is his aunt, only to learn that his aunt is actually African-American (Tung & Tong, 1995). In this way, Chan demonstrated his own faults, which, in turn, further humanized his character. Rather than subscribing to Lee's rigid racial preoccupation, Chan instead chose to adapt to a diverse society. By doing this, Chan immersed himself in the culture of the viewer, softening the Orientalist representations of Lee. Rather than playing the role of the victor in a victim narrative, Chan becomes a representative of China in the western world whose easy-going, nonalienating, and win–win approach to diversity is symbolic of China's emergence into neoliberal global capitalism.

Figure 5. Rumble in the Bronx, 1995

Not only did Chan represent a more well-rounded worldview, his own emotions and actions were far more rational than Lee's. For example, if Chan faced an entire dojo of trained Japanese fighters as Lee did *Fist of Fury*, he would have made the logical choice to avoid confrontation. In fact, a majority of the action in Chan's films concern him narrowly escaping swarms of adversaries through a variety of stunts and acrobatics. Chan typically only resorted to violence when necessary to protect himself, his friends, or his family. In this way, Chan presented himself as a problem solver, rather than a hotheaded vigilante whose actions were at the mercy of oppressing foreigners.

The role of women in Chan's films also stood in stark contrast to that of Lee's. In several of his movies, Jackie Chan has female sidekicks, who are equally as capable as him in a fight. In fact, women even had strong roles in his pre-American films, which took place in a pre-modern China. For example, in *Drunken Master II*, Chan's mother aids Jackie in deceiving his father, gambles, drinks, and refuses to shy away from violence (Tsang & Kar-leung, 1994). The equality between male and female figures in Chan's films stands in stark contrast to the hypermasculinity of Lee and the Cultural Revolution posters. Rather than needing to suppress femininity in order to demonstrate masculinity, Chan presents males and females as equal contributors (and patrons) to a globalized world. By utilizing both strong female characters and humor that drew attention to the weaknesses of filial piety, Chan dismissed archaic Chinese values and widened his global audience to reflect the modern treatment of women.

Chan's refusal to subscribe to Lee's caricature of hypermasculinity did not mean that he was not equally as masculine. Specifically, one major difference Chan implemented to the kung fu genre was the utilization of stunts. Like Lee, Chan refused to use special effects or stunt doubles, but he also extended the limits of the masculine body beyond choreographed fight scenes. Chan even included footage of his failed stunts during the credits of his movies, continuing to shatter the silver screen by showing the audience the exact amount of blood, sweat, and tears that are involved in his process (Tsang & Kar-leung, 1994). This behind-the-scenes look at filmmaking demonstrated not only Chinese advances in special effects (or lack thereof) and choreography, but also technology and industry.

Despite their promotion of the globality, plurality, and circulation of global capitalism, Chan's films are also aware of their negative aspects. This (ironically) further helps them to connect with his consumers. Just as Lee's resistance towards imperialism empathized with victims of oppression, Chan's films empathize with victims of global capitalism. For example, the gang members portrayed in *Rumble in the Bronx*, who are representatives of different American stereotypes, are forced to band together and operate in gangs in order to survive the hardships of capitalism. This also highlights the loss of power experienced by the individual citizens in both the American and Chinese governments. While the lottery-like game of global capitalism greatly benefits those who control it, the individual is left without the voice or power to fend for themself. Chan's portrayal of racial diversity also hides tension and competition which in turn highlights the hypocrisy of races who are pushed further and further together as globality increases. With an ironic sense of humor, Chan mocks the superficial success of global capitalism and therefore "socialism with Chinese characteristics" (Schoppa, 2011, p. 367).

By embodying modern transnational values, Chan foreshadowed and became symbolic of the rise of 21st century China. Similar to how Chan changed the perception of the Chinese by inserting himself into western culture and markets with a friendly face, "the PRC's speedy economic growth has bought it strategic, political, and commercial significance, all of which highlight its expanding relevance" (Wachman, 2011, p. 120). In comparison to the modern western action star, Chan stated,

> In American movie now, walking is special effect, talking is special effect, everything special effect. And American heroes never scared. Put a gun to their head, they say "shoot me, shoot me." But I'm not a superhero, I'm a real human being…[With special effects] you can be superwoman. You can lift a car up. That's special effects. Everybody can be a superman, but nobody can be a Jackie Chan. My body is my special effects. (Shu, 2003, p. 50)

This quote embodies his separation from Hollywood action stars. Chan confidently challenged western action stars because of the uniqueness of his product. Because of the high-demand of his films, Chan was able to find a unique niche in the western box-office.

While it is easy to perceive Chan's capture of the western box office, China's grasp on the global political field is just starting to reveal itself. Chan may not use special effects or smoke and mirrors in his work, but it seems as if China is ready to step out from behind the curtain. Chan's fighting style displayed in *Drunken Master* exemplifies this (Wachman, 2011). This style involves feigning drunkenness to trick the opponent into letting their guard down, upon which the kung fu master strikes. By remaining off-balance and "drunk," the kung fu master is able to "roll with the punches" and use their opponent's momentum for his own retaliation.

Despite Bruce Lee and Jackie Chan being cultural figures, their films are also symbolic of modern China's political changes. Therefore, the title of this paper, "*Fist of Fury* or *Drunken Master*," is an illustration of two different approaches to China's relationship with its own history. *Fist of Fury* confronts the trauma of the Century of Humiliation by presenting China with a hero within its victim narrative. By reinventing their masculine image, Bruce Lee was able to mend the previously shattered Chinese identity. As Deng Xiaoping began to ameliorate China from beyond this shame, cultural bandages and medicines became obsolete; instead, he worked to build upon China's new foundation (Schoppa, 2011). Despite western warnings of a Chinese threat often being derived from predictions of revenge against their imperial oppressors, Jackie Chan's *Drunken Master* made the entrance of the Chinese man onto the neoliberal global capital stage seamless and unintimidating to western society. China's emergence as a booming economy with a growing military force questions the supremacy of the western world. Now that China has successfully "bid its time," their display of wealth during the Olympic Games, economic mobility under "socialism with Chinese characteristics," and rapid military expansion signifies a return to the *Fist of Fury* of Bruce Lee as an attempt to resist and challenge the hegemony of Pax Americana (Schoppa, 2011, p. 367). While 21st century China has only begun to cement themselves as a global power, following the agile steps of Jackie Chan foreshadows its success on the international stage.

REFERENCES

Brownell, S. & Wasserstrom, J. N. (2002). *Chinese femininities, Chinese masculinities: A reader.* Berkeley, CA: University of California Press.

Chang, I. (1997). *The rape of Nanking: The forgotten holocaust of World War II.* New York, NY: BasicBooks.

Chin, F. (1974). Introduction: Fifty years of our whole voice. *Aiiieeeee! An anthology of Asian American writers.* Washington, DC: Howard University Press, xxi–xlviii.

Chow, R. (Producer), & Wei, L. (Director). (1971). *The big boss* [Motion picture]. Hong Kong: Golden Harvest.

Chow, R. (Producer) & Wei, L. (Director). (1972). *Fist of fury* [Motion picture]. Hong Kong: Golden Harvest.

Dai, G. (2011). The features and trend of the Chinese kung fu movie stars: Three case studies from Bruce Lee to Jackie Chan and Jet Li. *Journal of Beijing University of Physical Education, 6*(June*)*, 37-40, 53.

Fojas, C. (2011). New frontiers of Asian and Latino America in popular culture: Mixed-race intimacies and global police state in Miami Vice and Rush Hour 2. *Journal of Asian American studies, 14*(3), 417-434, 457. *doi:10.1353/jaas.2011.0031*

Gries, P. H. (2007). Narratives to live by: The century of humiliation and Chinese national identity today. In L. M. Johnson & T. B. Weston (Eds.), *China's transformations: The stories behind the headlines* (112-128). Lanham, MD: Rowman & Littlefield Publishers.

Hiramoto, M. (2012). Don't think, feel: Mediatization of Chinese masculinities through martial arts films. *Language & Communication, 32*(4), 386-399. doi:10.1016/j.langcom.2012.08.005

Kaufman, A. A. (2010). The 'century of humiliation,' then and now: Chinese perceptions of the international order. *Pacific Focus, 25*(1), 1-33. doi:10.1111/j.1976-5118.2010.01039.x

Lo, K. (1996). Muscles and subjectivity: A short history of the masculine body in Hong Kong popular culture. *Camera Obscura, 39*(9), 104-125. doi:10.1125/02705346-13

Shin, M. (2008). Yellow Hollywood: Asian martial arts in the U.S. global cinema (Doctoral dissertation). Retrieved from http://digitallibrary.usc.edu/cdm/ref/collection/p15799coll127/id/197116

Schoppa, K. (2011). Revolution and its past: Identities and change in modern Chinese history. Upper Saddle River, NJ: Prentice Hall. Pearson, 346.

Shu, Y. (2003). Reading the kung fu film in an American context: From Bruce Lee to Jackie Chan. *Journal of Popular Film and Television, 31*(2), 50-59. doi:10.1080/01956050309603666

sian gunn. (2014, July 19). *I am Bruce Lee documentary* [Video file]. Retrieved from https://youtu.be/ikCZ9piZspI

Teo, S. (2009). *Chinese martial arts cinema: The Wuxia tradition.* Edinburgh, Scotland: Edinburgh University Press.

Tsang, E. (Producer), & Kar-leung, L. (Director). (1994). *Drunken master II* [Motion picture]. Hong Kong: Golden Harvest.

Tung, B. (Producer), & Tong, S. (Director). (1995). *Rumble in the Bronx* [Motion picture]. Hong Kong: Golden Harvest.

Wachman, A. M. (2011). Why China gets a "rise" out of us: Ruminations on PRC foreign relations. In W. C. Kirby (Ed.), *The People's Republic of China at 60: An international assessment.* Cambridge, MA: Harvard University Press.

Wilson, D. (1982). *When tigers fight: The story of the Sino–Japanese War, 1937-1945.* New York, NY: Viking Press.

First Flame: An Interview with the Creators

Marley DeRosia

Real World Geneseo is a class in which participating students engage and challenge each other and themselves to explore issues related to social justice and privilege. Consisting of an intensive retreat and weekly academic seminars, one of the primary goals of the class is to provide students with the knowledge and skills necessary to become effective advocates for inclusivity. Based on their experiences in Real World Geneseo 2016, a group of six students worked with a number of collaborators to craft a spoken word performance (poetic verse designed to be read aloud) titled *First Flame*.

The six students behind *First Flame* were Nana Boakye, Elizabeth Boateng, Seung Kim, Jenny Soudachanh, Skyler Susnick, and Jawad (Momo) Tazari. The stories they told in their performance dealt with personal experiences with deeply-rooted societal expectations—from stereotypes that pigeonhole entire groups of people, to expectations of behavior based simply on appearance, to hope that something will change. Through their work, this diverse group of students show the courage to keep moving forward in a world that tries to hold them back. In *First Flame*, they let you know exactly who they are, what they think, and what they have been through.

The students worked with guest artist Mariposa Fernandez during a weekend retreat to create and hone a script for their eventual spoken word performance. The performance was directed by Dr. Mark Broomfield of the Department of Theatre and Dance, with accompanying music composed by Professor Glenn McClure.

I took the time to interview some of the individuals involved in the creation of *First Flame*, including Dr. Broomfield on his direction of the experience, Professor McClure on his experience writing the score, and the students who put their hearts on the line to write this piece. Through my questions, I hoped to unravel some of the motivations behind each individual's participation and shine a light on how one's experiences can be made into art.

An Interview with Dr. Mark Broomfield, Assistant Professor of Dance Studies

Sitting down and meeting with Dr. Broomfield, an interdisciplinary dancer with a passion for diversity, offered a fresh, wholesome take on what Real World Geneseo can do for students attending SUNY Geneseo. The 2016-2017 school year marks his fifth year at Geneseo, though this was only his first time leading Real World Geneseo. Through his work with the students and his interest in the project, Dr. Broomfield was able to support his students as they honed personal pieces and created a piece of art.

What made you want to get involved with this project?

Broomfield: I was an observer at the previous year's Real World Geneseo through their extreme learning program. This time marks my second time working with them but I was an observer the first time. I did participate, but I didn't want to fully immerse myself in order to get a sense for what the program was doing. The second year I fully immersed myself and facilitated; I worked with a lot of great people, Fatima Rodriguez Johnson (Assistant Dean of Students, Multicultural Programs & Service), Susan Norman (Director of the Xerox Center), and Glenn McClure (Professor of English). Even collaborating with the English department and Celia Easton (Dean of Academic Planning and Advising and Professor Of English) made it quite extensive in interdisciplinary work. They [Susan and Fatima] spear-headed the project and I was able to see the full scope of what the program does during the intensive weekend retreat the students went on.

The diversity of the program drew me in: it's rich, it's so rich. That's what attracted me to it too. You can see in Geneseo, an institution with thousands of people, that programs like this have an impact, particularly in those students' lives. Bringing the guest artist in was new and we thought it would be a great fit. I wanted to work with Mariposa before and this just felt like a great way to also build on what the dance department does; the spoken word didn't adhere to dance as we typically know of dance performance and I'm all about open access. Everybody can write and tell their story. That, in terms of a threshold to the stage, you couldn't ask for anything more. We wanted students from diverse backgrounds to offer their perspectives that wouldn't normally be on that stage.

What's your take on Real World Geneseo?

Broomfield: It's quite powerful. It's called an "extreme learning course" and I think it does great work. I think all students should go through it. It's limited to about thirty students, but all students should go through it. With all the issues we're thinking about currently, nationwide, issues of diversity, inclusivity, there's no question that this should be a class that all students should have access to. The testimonies of student participants always discuss it as transformational; they're not the same after. It's just doing such important work. The makeup of the students is mostly diverse; I think so much of the young generation today relies on content, your education, but no one is teaching you how to live. No one is teaching you how to relate to other people. You can't have assumptions about the way we relate to other people. We come from various backgrounds of all kinds, and that's what is revealed in the retreat: the diversity and their perspectives. If you don't have a space to facilitate inside classes that don't coincide with real issues happening outside, they still impact what goes on inside the class. Part of the reason students want to participate is so they have a space to talk about these issues, because, by and large, they don't have a space to do that on campus that affirms where they come from or their marginalization: race, sexuality, gender identity, whether or not you're an immigrant—we have many students who go through many experiences that the program works with.

What was the structure of the course for students involved?

Broomfield: Six students were involved with the final performance. The max number of students in the course was thirty. It was focused around students that showed an interest and there were two different tracks the course could take: one was the performance track or they could take the course without the performance component, where they had to do service instead. That weekend that Mariposa was here was very intense and we created the performance literally from scratch. It wouldn't have existed without Mariposa. She created the environment for all the students' experiences to emerge the way that they did; writing autobiographically through writing prompts, we created a script in the week following the retreat as the students worked directly with Mariposa. Getting feedback from her and their peers was courageous.

Did you have any expectations going into the project?

Broomfield: I had no expectations. I didn't even know who I'd be working with. I had a vision of what I wanted to accomplish, but I wanted to see where the project could go. I didn't know what we were going to do. That's what creativity is, that's what theatre is. You get into an empty studio and you create, you play, you make something happen out of nothing. They had to trust the director and trust the guest artist but many students wanted to see where this project would take them and it was a risk. They weren't familiar and they were worried but when the performance occurred, the students were transformed. It was a testament to their courage too, to go on stage and perform. There were quite a few vulnerable stories. Because of the topics—it wasn't wildly controversial—but it was definitely for an adult audience, we were dealing with adult material. We got feedback that people loved it, but dance and performance come in many forms. People asked, "Why is there spoken word in a dance performance?" but it's about a destroying the barrier to access for students that don't normally have the opportunity to go onstage. They were completely welcomed by the dance students and it was a mutually inspirational process between the speakers and the dancers. That's what interdisciplinary work does. Everybody is affected by doing the work, and to witness that was like, "Wow." For myself certainly, it was great. To see where the students started, to witness the process and later, the reward, it was affirming.

Would you like to lead a class like this again?

Broomfield: We should clearly do more of this. I would love to lead a class like this again. It's like Safe Zone training, everyone should experience it. You can be exposed to different perspectives and you learn to question assumptions you may have about other people and yourself. It's an important contribution on campus with diversity being such a critical component at this time nationally. It's even more important for the institution to continue to show their support and bring awareness to issues people might not be aware of.

What other GREAT Day projects have you done in the past?

Broomfield: It's usually an outgrowth of what the students are doing in class. Last year, we did dance eth-nographies and one group presented on Kaplan's tai chi class, and they put so much work into it, we had to put it in GREAT Day. In the fall, classes consist of student-choreographed works and in the spring, it's faculty and guest artists, so it's a mix of the outgrowth of what our students do. GREAT Day is a chance for students to present their work, but last year, I wanted the students to interpret faculty's work. They might have been dancing to someone else's work, but it was about the process: what they learned even though they didn't make it. It's a wonderful opportunity to have the students interpret. Just like you read someone else's work and interpret it and write an essay to present to the audience, we're doing the same thing, we're just performing it. It's requiring them to think in a different way even though it took them time to see that distinction; that it's still about you, not about the faculty. People are coming to see you and what you do, how you interpret it. You can speak about the history, the culture, or whatever in the process that you were learning it.

This year, I'm creating a choreographic duet for the dance concert—a spiritual—and I think it's an excellent opportunity for students to talk about the process and what interpretation of a work needs.

AN INTERVIEW WITH GLENN MCCLURE, ADJUNCT PROFESSOR OF ENGLISH

Glenn McClure's expertise and professionalism shined through as I interviewed him regarding his experience with *First Flame* and past GREAT Days. Providing a wonderful score that dipped, moved, and danced through the performance along with the stories of the actors, Professor McClure's pride for his college and the students involved resonated during the interview.

How did you get involved with this class's performance?

McClure: Dr. Broomfield attended one of my presentations and later asked me if I was interested in working with *First Flame*. After he described a multi-disciplinary, collaborative, artistic exploration of big issues affecting Geneseo students, it was easy to say "yes."

How did you choose the music that would be utilized in the performance?

McClure: My musical contribution was created with the same process as the script and dance. I participated in early visioning sessions surrounding student writing pieces. I responded to the spoken word with music, but like any other creative process, the first draft wasn't very good. As the writing and dance evolved, so did my musical responses. This was not a top-down process. It was a lateral collaboration with the students, professors, and guest artists.

What kind of collaborations have you done within SUNY Geneseo in the past?

McClure: I have a long history with Geneseo. As an undergraduate, I played in the String Band, Jazz Ensemble, Wind Ensemble, and Chamber Singers. I also played both on and off stage in several musical theater productions. Over the years, my collaborative work with the college has stretched beyond pure artistic projects to include helping develop study abroad experiences in Ghana and Nicaragua, philanthropic work for a variety of regional charities, work with the migrant center, writing grants with the Sponsored Research Office, and more. I am happy to be part of the Geneseo community in a variety of capacities.

What are some of your favorite memories from past GREAT Days?

McClure: The key note address by my friend and colleague, Dava Sobel, was a highlight, but as a professor, I am always partial to the presentations of my students. These have ranged from health initiatives in rural Nicaragua to teaching Humanities with great music. GREAT Day is one of the best ideas we have ever had. It is so refreshing to hand the college over to the students for a day, while the professors sit, listen, and learn.

Professor McClure closed the interview with the following statement:

SUNY Geneseo's reputation as a top-notch liberal arts college shines through in projects like *First Flame*. This may not be the thing that ends up in our college marketing materials. It may not be the first thing the

president mentions in state wide forums, but it does represent the best of what we try to do here. *First Flame* pushed students and professors to ask deep, difficult questions about ourselves and our community. It was joyously self-critical, functioning under the assumption that a challenge to our assumptions is an opportunity to understand more deeply what we really believe. The performance, while guided by faculty and our guest artist, was driven by the participating students. Their exploration of racism, sexism, miscommunication, resilience, perseverance, justice, and hope was at the same time beautiful and unsettling. They did not create artwork that preached a point of view. They smashed stereotypes with personal narratives that demanded their audience's attention (and mine as their composer). Their work confronted our culture's increasing acceptance of the notion that unfiltered thought is somehow more authentic than deep, careful, thoughtful, and patient artistic creation. These students did more than "like" an unsubstantiated Facebook post or "unfriend" someone who challenges their assumptions. They followed the long, uncertain path necessary to creating art that matters today and endures for years to come. This is the kind of art that is truly authentic and subscribes to no cliché or easy slogan or ideology. They did the stuff that goes way beyond our test scores, our awards, or our college rankings. These students are the real deal. I was proud to be with them on a small part of their journey.

AN INTERVIEW WITH THE STUDENTS OF *FIRST FLAME*

What inspired you to write this piece?

Elizabeth Boateng: The inspiration came from a series of writing prompts that Mariposa gave us. One prompt included writing three words that described us, then having one minute of free writing to expand on the prompt. We then worked together to edit our writing into this final piece.

Jenny Soudachanh: There were several different aspects of the piece that I had written on my own, but I also collaborated with my group members as well as Mariposa who tied our thoughts into one big piece. I drew my inspiration from the RWG7 [Real World Geneseo 7] retreat I attended. I thought about how society ignores many different -isms (racism, classism,

sexism, etc.) when it does not impact them directly. Another case is that it is easier to ignore differences and pretend they do not exist or are unaware of how they exist. I wanted to express that this isn't an issue that has been solved yet.

As I went through the retreat, I remembered my own upbringing in New York City: how segregated the city can be but also how accepting it may be. It was easier for me to relate with people who had been exposed to diversity because I had been through something similar. I had thought I knew everything there was to know about diversity but this retreat proved to me how wrong I was, how I had unconsciously participated in acting on stereotypes. I chose to speak about my own experiences because I wanted to inform individuals of the subtle things that can be discriminatory as well as the big things; because continuous small jabs over a lifetime can hurt just as much, or even more, than one huge punch.

Skyler Susnick: I wanted to share my story. I wanted to expose people to a variety of stories that they may have not heard before.

Obviously, this is a very personal piece: how did you feel expressing yourself in such an intimate way?

Elizabeth: At first I was hesitant to be open and honest, especially with the writing prompts. But once I realized my words were important, and my voice would be heard, it was easier to share my intimate thoughts.

Jenny: It was completely intimate, horrifying, and vulnerable in every sense. There were many different aspects I felt that I had never fully expressed to others until I wrote it on paper and had to say it out loud. However, the group made it a safe space and Mariposa had encouraged this expression—to speak out because we all matter. It was validating.

Skyler: It was very nerve wracking. By expressing myself in such an intimate way, I felt very exposed. It was also very exciting and, in a way, liberating to be so open about personal things in such a public way.

Did you expect to create something like this at the start of the class? How did you feel jumping into this project?

Elizabeth: I had no idea that I would be performing or publishing my work at the beginning of class. I was under the impression that the performance would be choreographed and that the lines would just be fed to me. So, I was kind of blindly jumping into this project since this was the first time a project like this was done at SUNY Geneseo.

Jenny: I had not expected such an intimate piece, as our first couple of writing prompts did not go as in-depth as our final project. However, as we kept writing throughout the project, they became deeper, more intimate, and more revealing to each individual's feelings and psyche that we may not have known at first glance.

Skyler: I expected to create and perform a spoken word piece at the start of the class, but not quite like what we did. It really altered and exceeded the expectations I had at the beginning of the class. I felt excited and a little wary jumping into this project, not really knowing what to expect.

Have you had any experience in theatre before? How did this affect the process of writing and performing the piece?

Elizabeth: I've had experience with theater in high school performing small parts. It somewhat affected the process, but I wasn't consciously writing with audience entertainment in mind.

Jenny: I had experience in theatre in elementary school and middle school, however, I started to develop stage fright in middle school because of a mistake I made during a school play, thus I started to stay away from it. At Geneseo I worked as a TA for Johnnie Ferrell for four years in his technical theater class. I think that because I was already so familiar with the stage, this project wasn't as daunting of a task, but I was still nervous. Every night right before our performance, I would have to remind myself to breath in deeply, to remember that if I could hold onto the emotions and my beliefs, then the words would always come to me.

I love to write, so it was wonderful for me to be able to express myself through this process. I enjoyed the self-expression on paper, how liberating it felt to write about topics that aren't the norm. However, sometimes during the performance, the writing is exaggerated. There's a visual aid of how the speaker is portraying their story. It was a little awkward when it wasn't my piece and I had to act in it; I always felt a little ridiculous at times when I had to exaggerate, but I knew it also had to happen to have an impact.

Skyler: I had done some improv in high school with a group that tackled the issues that teens face using a combination of humor and more serious conversations, which was definitely the lens through which I entered this project. I think it made me more comfortable performing and being so open with the people I worked with and our audience.

Do you wish you did anything differently?

Elizabeth: I wish I wrote about different experiences.

Jenny: I wish I had taken a more proactive role in making our performances more known.

Skyler: I don't think I would do anything differently.

How did working with Mariposa Fernandez aid the creative process? What was it like working with her?

Elizabeth: As I stated earlier, Mariposa guided our writing with her prompts. Working with her was really amazing, she had the ability to spark a flame I didn't realize I had. Especially with prepping for the actual performance. She helped us gain confidence and stage presence.

Jenny: Mariposa is an inspiring individual who helped me find the confidence to express my voice. She encouraged us to express ourselves and validated our experiences. I felt empowered after our sessions together where I learned a lot about how to purposefully use my body to convey my emotions to others. She said that she wanted to hear more about our stories and that other people should know about our experiences.

Skyler: Working with Mariposa was instrumental to my creative process. She had many prompts to get us writing, and her encouragement gave me the confidence to write in ways I never would have been able to otherwise. Working with Mariposa was an incredible experience I feel very lucky to have had.

How do you think people will feel reading this piece, or seeing it performed? What was the message you hoped to get across to the audience?

Elizabeth: There wasn't an exact reaction I expected from the audience. The message I hoped to convey was that we can all relate to each other within our different life experiences.

Jenny: As diverse as Geneseo is, there are still cases of prejudice that exist though people may not realize it. Stereotypes, microaggressions, and biases still exist on campus and I believe many people sweep it under the rug. However, denying it is invalidating. I think if a person wants to truly be empathetic and really understand another's background and diversity, they have to sit in that discomfort and face it. So, granted, there were some nights where we were well-received by the audiences. During some performance nights, there were cheers, sassy positive comments, and applause. I remember strangers telling me that they enjoyed the performance, and that it was the most unique performance they'd ever seen. But other nights, it was quiet and we could see how uncomfortable the audience became. But they sat through it and watched it, and I hope they understood the message we were trying to send.

My own message aimed to target the micro-aggressions and biases I have faced in the past, including during the time I've spent at SUNY Geneseo. I am a mix of Laotian and Chinese, but I was born and raised in New York City. I've faced biases and stereotypes from my professors who assumed I was an international student, from those that assume I can speak for an entire culture when topics of race come up, and from other students who tell me that I "speak English very well." These small things can seem harmless and may have good intentions, but they can build and make a person feel unwanted—like a foreigner, like an "other." I wanted people to recognize these microaggressions and be conscious of it. I wanted to make a statement of awareness.

Skyler: To me, the purpose of the piece was to expose the audience to new and different identities and stories. I think people are all more alike than different but it can be very important and powerful to share life experiences that they may not have had. I know I loved hearing the stories of the other cast members and I hope the audience liked it as well. I hope they learned something from hearing our stories.

First Flame

Created by Mariposa Fernandez
Written and Performed by Nana Boakye,
Elizabeth Boateng, Seung Kim, Jenny Soudachanh,
Skyler Alexander Susnick, and Jawad (Momo) Tazari
Music by Glenn McClure
Directed and Choreographed by Dr. Mark Broomfield

CAST OF CHARACTERS

Nana: College-aged, African man. Comes from a lower-middle class, two parent household in downstate New York. Finds motivation in performing.

Liz: College-aged, Ghanaian-American woman from the Bronx. Raised in a single-parent home with four siblings.

Seung: Korean-American, college-aged man with an aptitude for languages.

Jenny: Graduate student, Asian, cis-gender female. Born the youngest to two refugees in Queens, New York. Dedicated to supporting equity and fighting stereotypes by making intersectionality and individuality known to others.

Skyler: College-aged, white, gay, transgender man. Comes from an upper-middle class, single-parent household in Connecticut. Easy going and sincere.

Momo: College-aged man. Vegetarian and activist.

I. Journey into Spaces and Sounds

SETTING: Urban street scene

[Cast enters theater from multiple entrance points. The percussionist begins to set the tone for the scene, musically. Eventually all members of the ensemble converge on blocks, stage right.]

NANA
My story walks out onto the open space and takes it all in.

SEUNG
Let me take you to a place where the heavy, humid heat of the sun beats down bricks of sweat onto my neck.

JENNY
I want to take you to a place where bright red cherry tomatoes sprout from their vines, where children in a grassy backyard run around a small tree not much bigger than themselves.

LIZ
I wanna take you to a place where the city folk are never smiling but go home and transform into the warmest, kindhearted people.

MOMO
Where the trees are tall and animals walk among the humans, stinky, wild chickens, and floral banana trees.

JENNY
Where the sun shines onto the pavement and where small feet slam against the ground in excitement.

LIZ
I wanna take you to a place where the streets are cold, where the youth cling to.

SKYLER
A place where I grew up. A place for "fringe kids." A place filled with the sounds of video games and music.

LIZ
Where you can't escape the loud sounds of the 4 train.

NANA
The fruits are free for everyone to pick. Money isn't the key to survival.

JENNY
I want to take you to a place where mothers in their yellow, flowing sundresses holler at their children to be careful.

SKYLER

A place on the edge of the town's main stretch, in an old town building, a big open one made for trucks or salt or something.

JENNY

Where fathers are relaxing on chairs and sipping damp, condensing beers.

[Musical transition]

NANA

Where I'm from, you're either in or out so get with the program. There is no middle. Normally people think for themselves but in this place if you don't look like us then, "Homie, you needs to bounce."

LIZ

Where I'm from boys tap their knees, give life to the story of their weekly chase-down by cops from the 40th precinct.

SEUNG

한국에서 태어나서 한국인인데

I grew up in New York so I'm a New Yorker.

근데 뉴욕에서는 사람들이 나를 한국인으로 보고

And Koreans see me as an American.

But I'm really not either.

日本語も喋るけど、日本人じゃなくて

Je parle français mais je ne suis pas français.

Ik spreek een beetje Nederlands maar ik kom niet uit Nederland.

I'm all of these things together.

I'm just me damn it. I'm just me.

LIZ

Where I'm from you wouldn't survive a day. You better know which streets not to walk down when it's dark.

JENNY

I'm from screams of anger! Pleas of apologies and mercy are yelled across tiny matchbox-like rooms. I'm from subways and rails, where rats scurry and the odor of piss lingers in the air. Where I'm from—

SKYLER

—was just a means for me to get here, where I want to be. I'm all about my horizontal identities and communities. My vertical ones are secondary. Family of blood and family of choice.

MOMO

Where I am from is not where I've lived. It's a realm of abstraction, of unity, of all creation. Not a place of division and discrimination, but solidarity and acceptance.

II. SELF-DISCLOSURES

[Musical transition]

NANA

Is having pride really that bad? I'm great. I'm reaching for the sky.

Cameras and flashing lights.

Kanye moments and quiet arenas as I drop the mike.

[Pause]

Recognize me when I walk.

MOMO

The world is crafted by how we act.

Because when you are assaulted, I am also attacked.

Humans alone do not experience pain.

Because all life on earth suffers for material gain.

[Pause and cross stage]

Because I like chicken, but not on my plate.

I love animals, not how they taste.

Because to kill for profit is unjust.

I do not consume carcass.

LIZ

Because she knows she can be great, and she will prove it to the world.

Where detrimental cycles are destined for people who look like her.

Bright minds tainted by the fast life.

Scamming and pushing weight on Bronx street corners.

She was raised by the true head of household who bears generations.

Optimistic in a world that denies her integration.

She is me.

And I refuse to allow my inner lioness to lose sleep over the opinion of sheep.

I shoot for the stars.

[out to the audience]

Never settle for the moon.

SKYLER

Because some days I could hardly look in the mirror.

Because there were times where sex turned into crying in Kyle's arms.

Because I wanted to love my body as much as my boyfriend does.

Because it was time to become myself.

To be reborn into my truer form.

Like a phoenix from its ashes.

I got top surgery.

JENNY

Because as a smile blooms on her face.

While rough, cracked skin grazes my collarbone.

My mother hands it to me.

Like a heavy chain that binds me to my family.

Because it reminds me.

Of applause and cheers in a room where shoulders brush together.

Laughter, hugs, tears.

And goodbyes.

Forever against my skin.

Because it is valued yet forgotten.

Because every time I come home.

I enter a warm embrace.

I wear the comforting necklace my mother gave me.

Everyday.

SEUNG

Because I was bullied for my weight,

Because I was vulnerable,

Because I was defenseless,

I spent hours and hours.

Worrying.

Freaking out, depressed, alone.

Crying myself to sleep.

Until one day,

A light bulb went off.

Why did I care so much?

Why did I need to listen to them?

I accept myself for who I am.

No more crying myself to sleep.

No more depression.

No more insecurities.

No more loneliness.

No more worrying.

No more anything else.

But just being me,

I don't care what you think of me.

>SETTING: *Campus / The Green*
>
>*[Conversational scene, structured improvisation, ensemble interacts with each other & audience]*

NANA

I don't want to hear that everyone in Africa is dirty, hungry, and poor.

SKYLER

I'm getting sick of being asked my old name.

SEUNG

Don't say that Asian men aren't good looking or that we can't be manly.

LIZ

Yo! I'm tired of hearing black girls are only good in bed.

MOMO

Muslims are not Terrorists. Islam is not a religion of hate.

SEUNG

Stop getting surprised at how "good" my English is. I've lived here for over 15 years.

JENNY

Seriously, don't ask if I grew up with an Asian tiger mom.

>*[Overlapping dialogue, ensemble begins to interrupt each other, build up to a crescendo]*

NANA

I am not wrong.

SEUNG

I matter and I exist.

LIZ

I need to hear only my voice in my head.

JENNY

Ask questions free of assumptions.

SKYLER

I'm valid.

MOMO

I want to hear that we challenge our assumptions every day.

ENSEMBLE

LISTEN!!!

NANA

I don't wanna hear it!

III. THIS STORY IS GONNA BURN

[Musical transition]

JENNY

I can tell you a story that's a cold spaghetti dinner eaten with chopsticks or a story that's hot like fire.

LIZ

This story is gonna burn you.

> *[Liz continues to say this line, rhythmically in sync with live percussion]*

SEUNG

I want the story to burn me, to leave behind a mark.

SKYLER

I want the story to burn me. I want the story to burn me and give me chills.

NANA

I want the story to burn me. Like the accidental touch of an iron that has been left on too long.

SKYLER

The story of pain and struggle.

NANA

Like your first college breakup. Like your first failing grade.

MOMO

I want the story to burn you; I want you to feel the fire of the gathered crowd, the emotion in the spoken chant, the bitter taste of the mist of pepper spray.

SKYLER

The story of finding yourself in an unwelcoming world.

SEUNG

I want it to mark its territory.

I want it to stick and never let go.

MOMO

This story is going to burn you, because it is the truth. The truth hurts, and coming in contact with reality is scary, really scary.

SKYLER

The story of losing someone.

Someone you love.

Someone you need.

Maybe yourself.

MOMO

It says everything you have been afraid to express, and uncomfortable to hear.

NANA

I want the story to burn you. Like your skin rubbing against the track when you take that hard fall to the finish.

MOMO

That's good. It's good that you are uncomfortable, because things need to change.

SEUNG

Only when you're scorched,

Can you finally learn.

Restaurant Scene written by Seung Kim

SETTING: New York City sushi restaurant

[Musical transition. Seung narrates, Momo plays Jeremy, Nana plays Arthur]

SEUNG

Remember when we had sushi in the city with Arthur? And he kept on making racist jokes, comments on my facial features and lewd remarks about certain body parts. He never had sushi before, and neither did you, Jeremy. So when you went to the bathroom, I told Arthur to eat the entire portion of wasabi with his sushi roll. As soon as he opened his mouth to eat, I got excited. I was finally going to teach this racist motherfucker a lesson. But instead, as soon as he closed his mouth with the wasabi penetrating all of his taste buds, he began to scream and gag. Then, he threw up. I ran out of there, onto W. 55th street, struggling to catch my breath. When I went back inside, you had just come out of the bathroom, and you looked at me and said:

JEREMY

Seung! What have you done?

SEUNG

I felt guilty but in a sense, I also felt proud even though I hurt Arthur. Sorry, but not sorry.

Party Scene written by Nana Boakye

[Lights dim. Musical transition to an upbeat tempo. Ensemble breaks to the beat. Laughin', dancin', groovin', highfivin'. Liz and Skyler act out the roles of desired woman and close friend, as Nana narrates]

NANA

It was dark, the music was playing and everyone was dancing, moving to the sound of the beat. One of my closest friends made his way from the dance floor over to me and told me that he had spotted a girl that he really wanted to dance with. She was cute and I knew if I grabbed her she wouldn't turn me down. As he went on and on about how he should approach her, I just thought to myself, "Now would be the perfect time to seek my revenge." A couple of months earlier, he had gotten with a girl that I had told him I liked. He probably didn't know how serious I felt about the girl but it didn't matter to me. I began to plot in my head: now was the perfect opportunity to get my revenge. As he made his way over, I followed him quietly. Stalking him like a lion stalking its prey. I moved through the sea of people ever so smoothly so he wouldn't notice my presence. As he began talking to her, I reached over his shoulder and gently grabbed her hand. I slowly pulled her close and she offered no resistance. We began grinding to the music while he stood there in shock. Not because of what I did, but because it actually worked. 'Cause I'm smooth.

IV. REBEL REALNESS

Party scene continued, written by Liz Boateng

[Musical transition to a slow tempo]

LIZ

Who doesn't enjoy the soft sounds of intimacy.

The heat created as two people become one in a private embrace.

Small drops of sweat running down your spine.

As you encounter the overly pursued sense of pleasure.

LIZ & JENNY

They warn you it'll hurt at first.

LIZ

But you are blindly struck by vulnerability.

The taste of yearning for more.

Constantly lingering over your head.

As you wonder why you had help in the revelation of your nakedness.

But you're left to dress yourself.

When it's all over.

Monologue written by Skyler Alexander Susnick

SETTING: Supercuts

[Ensemble forms a line. Sklyer stage right. Sklyer speaks, cast is posing and checking themselves out in an imaginary mirror]

SKYLER

My mother still misses her daughter.

I remember my first haircut after coming out like it was yesterday. I was terrified walking into Supercuts, for all appearances a teenage girl with a flat chest and masculine clothing. My hair was shoulder length at the time and I had a picture on my phone of a guy with a haircut I liked, longish but masculine. I showed the haircutter and she started. In the end it was still a little more feminine than I would have cared for, but I was too nervous to say anything and I liked it well enough anyway. For the first time in years I recognized myself when I looked in the mirror, something I hadn't even realized I was missing. I sat in my car in the parking lot and just looked at it in the mirror. If I was the type to cry out of happiness I would have.

Monologue written by Jenny Soudachanh

[Musical transition]

JENNY

Eyes and mouths everywhere.

From the moment I pop out of the womb.

To the moment I crawl and walk always saying.

You should do this and you should do that.

At home, on the street, in books, in classrooms, on TV.

Expectations and entitlement.

Pulling me, dragging me.

Hands that cover my eyes, turn into lenses.

Chains made of lace pull me forward.

But I cannot follow as expected.

When I discover there is a world beyond the screen on my eyes.

When I question: why do I have to do this? Is this really me?

I stumble on purpose, make you pause and look back.

Why must I fantasize about another road I could have taken, a world not my own?

Why must I reflect on possibilities I could have taken?

But rejected because I believed them when they said, "That's not for you."

I want you to watch me, scream at me.

As I sever the rope and walk away,

As I choose to open my own mouth and look at the world with my own eyes.

I can do this and that.

I'm not who you make me out to be.

I'm not that someone.

I can do this.

> SETTING: Starting line of a race
>
> [Shift: Cast uses imaginary line, looking back in anticipatory poses, waiting for the baton, Finally, they break into cheering]

ENSEMBLE

[Whispering]

I can do this. I can do this.

JENNY

It hurts to inhale through your nose as sweat drips down your chin. There and—

ENSEMBLE

Keep going!

JENNY

But it hurts as the fatigue slowly seeps into your warming body.

ENSEMBLE

You can do it!

NANA

You've taken thousands of steps and each one carries a different memory. Then the instant replay. You fight to cross the finish line. Everything becomes a blur and all you can hear are the screams.

ENSEMBLE

Come on Nana you're almost there!

Move Nana he's right behind you!

Try to catch him, he's right in front of you!

NANA

You cross the line using every ounce of energy left in you. As you reach out for the medal you snap back to reality and just catch yourself reaching for air. Just distant memories now. Just tighten your laces and begin your warm up for the race ahead of you.

JENNY

The sun beats down on your skin creating hot sweat. Desperation streams out of your pores. But you slam your foot into the ground with your never-give-up spirit, feel the heavy weight of your body move forward, 'til you hit the finish line.

> *[Pause and out to audience]*

Don't stop.

> *[Musical transition, percussive hip hop beat, interactive call and response, cast members engage audience, clapping as they walk off stage and through the house]*

NANA

Now when I say don't, y'all say stop!

NANA

Don't!

ENSEMBLE

Stop!

NANA

Don't!

ENSEMBLE

Stop!

NANA

When I say won't, y'all say stop!

NANA

Won't!

ENSEMBLE

Stop!

NANA

Won't!

ENSEMBLE

Stop!

[Ongoing chant as they exit]

FIN

www.ingramcontent.com/pod-product-compliance
Lightning Source LLC
Chambersburg PA
CBHW081250040426

42452CB00015B/2778